THE BIRDS & THE LILIES

THE BIRDS

& THE LILIES

WHAT IF THERE IS ANOTHER WAY THAN WORRY AND ANXIETY?

written by

Willow Weston

All biblical references are from the NIV
unless otherwise noted.

info@wecollide.net

Cover and book design by Lindsey Kiniry

First printing edition 2018
wecollide.net

Table of Contents

The Collide Story

I remember walking into a counseling office over a decade ago because my pain was chasing me down. I had run into Jesus and had even been leading in ministry for years prior to walking in for help, but God was inviting me into a deeper healing than I had yet to receive and perhaps a higher calling than I had yet to understand. I walked in for guidance because my pain was leaking out in ways that scared me. I sat in that counselor's office and stared at her clock as she asked me the all too expected question: "So what brings you in here today?"

I had a run-in with Jesus Christ in that office that had nothing to do with the counselor. God gave me two words: wounded collision. He helped me to see that I was born into pain. I had collided with wounds that were never healed, and they wounded me and now I wounded others. Sometimes it seems like we are all bumping around, colliding and wounding each other. I sat in that room desperate for all of us to have a new kind of collision. My pain was crying out for it.

When I see Jesus, He collides with people and rather than wounding them, He leaves them more whole. God's Spirit showed up in that counseling office in a way that pierced the air. God invited me to see those who wounded me from His perspective rather than my own. God called me to enter people's brokenness, instead of running from it. God reminded me that He is, indeed, a God who wipes brokenness all over Himself. I was being invited to collide with Jesus in my brokenness and invite others to come along.

So, I walked out of that appointment holding a spiritual concept, but even more, I knew in my innards that I was being called to do something big with those two words. Soon afterwards a beautiful young college aged girl from church asked if I would mentor her. I wasn't feelin' like the mentoring type right about then. She said she wanted to learn more about Jesus. I invited her to get together and study the Bible and see what happens when Jesus collides with wounded people. She was excited, so excited, that she invited all her friends, because twenty-some college women came knocking on my door.

We spent the next several years looking at Jesus colliding with people in the New Testament and as we did, He collided with us too. When Jesus restored the shriveled man's hand, He too, restored these college girls' shriveled self-esteems. When Jesus said to the woman caught in the act of adultery, "Go and sin no more", He too, said this to the young woman in my living room who had been caught stark naked in shame and Jesus set her free. When Jesus went out of His way to collide with the woman at the well who was going from man to man to man because she was so thirsty, Jesus too, met the college girls in my living room and He gave them something to drink that quenched their parched living. Those twenty girls and I experienced a new kind of collision when we ran into Jesus, one that brought about wholeness.

Most of the girls graduated and moved away from college. There were four girls left and they wanted to keep meeting. I prayed, and God said, "I am not into us 4 and no more Bible studies, it's time they teach the message." I was working as a college minister at the time and this idea came out of nowhere. I had a lot of other things on my plate, not to mention a full-time job, a husband and two kids. God handed us an opportunity to do something to impact lives that was beyond our understanding, but we had to act on His invitation. So, we did an experiment and that experiment led to what is now Collide, this ministry, that invites women of all ages, races, socioeconomic statuses, faith backgrounds, and life places to run into Jesus and as they do, they are forever transformed.

God took a story of pain and brokenness and turned it into this beautiful ministry we call Collide. We shape and craft events, conferences and retreats for thousands of women every year. We now have a counseling program assisting people who desire to walk towards healing in their life. We encourage and support mentoring, where women meet in life changing intergenerational relationships and co-learn from one another. We have a blog that God is using to invite people all around the country to collide with Jesus. We have a podcast which encourages women weekly with engaging content that is reflective of Jesus' love for them. We have a leadership and ministry development program where we are inviting women to tap into God's purpose for their lives. We have a church bridging program partnering with many local churches in the hopes of inviting women to walk a bridge from our events into the local church, so they will keep colliding. We have an amazing staff of gifted passionate, fierce women who are giving their lives away for this mission. And in 2018, we launched our Bible studies which we are creating and sharing in the hopes that more and more people will run into Christ.

I am continually amazed by this Jesus who shows up right smack dab in the midst of our mess and pain and walks us into healing and purpose. Collide has become a place, a community, a movement for so many to run into Jesus just as they are. My hope is that in the same way God met me years ago when I most needed it, He too will meet you right where you find yourself. He is a God who collides... so get ready because He does incredible, big, mighty, miraculous, unimaginable things when you run into Him.

founder and director of Collide

Collide Values

We value women colliding with Jesus and His teachings.

We value and encourage authenticity (telling our story as it really is).

We value recognizing brokenness, so it can be made whole.

We value the experience and support that comes from an intergenerational community of women of all ages, church backgrounds, life experiences, and faith stages.

We value teaching a theology that runs into the holistic parts of who we are, to encourage a healthy spirituality.

We value pushing towards growth and next steps to go further on one's journey with God.

We value challenging, equipping and inspiring people to serve, lead, minister and use their gifts in order to live into their God-given purpose and change lives.

Collide invites people of all ages, stages, experiences and faith backgrounds, as imperfect or broken as they may be on their journey, to authentically run into Jesus; as He collides with them, they are forever transformed.

Collide Mission

Who we are
and who we aren't

We are everyday chicks running into Jesus. This Bible study was written, researched and created by ordinary women of all ages, stages and backgrounds, desiring to know God. We have indigestion, PMS, anxiety, and bad hair days. We work jobs, serve on PTA boards, sit on church committees, coach sports and attempt to bless our neighbors. We have different skin colors, different generational experiences, different faith backgrounds and different economic statuses. We like Cheetos and red wine, candles, a good book and a walk on the beach. We get insecure and let fear get in our way sometimes. We battle and wrestle and pray and pray. We have bills to pay, kids to raise, relationships to reconcile and big dreams we'd like to see become reality. We are your neighbors, your friends, your everyday women.

We are not Bible scholars. We have not been to Seminary. We don't have a lot of letters after our name. We don't speak Hebrew or Greek. We are not all that impressive in "religious" circles. If you are looking for that kind of Bible study resource, there are so many great ones, and this might not be the one for you. We merely desire God and are mesmerized by Jesus. We want to learn, grow, study and be challenged and inspired by who God is and who He calls us to be. It is this desire that has led us to run into Jesus and to invite others to come along.

We are still in the midst of our story. We are in chapter 6, not at the end of the book. We have not "arrived." God's not done with us. What we think, feel, or believe might transform, morph, or reconstruct as God continues to collide with us. Who we are now and who we are becoming leaves room for us to be in process, to seek, to ask questions and to be God's kids. We believe God is the best Author and He writes the best story and the story that He is writing in your life and ours is being written as we speak... and so we engage His best story and trust Him for chapter 8, chapter 9 and so on.

We don't have all the answers. We did not set out to write Bible studies because we think we have the Holy Bible nailed down. We do not think we know the answers to all the questions. We don't think we can solve age-old theological debates nor current hot button arguments. We don't think we are tighter with the Big Man upstairs and therefore can tell you all that you need to know. All we know for sure is that God is alive and well. He loves us, and He shows just how much He loves us in Jesus Christ. We know for sure that God desires to collide with us and when we do we are forever transformed. Because we don't have all the answers, we are okay with inviting you, our friends, to come with us as we collide with Jesus together. We don't feel the pressure to be know-it-alls, experts or professional "Christians". Neither do we feel we need to provide you with all the answers, easy answers, formulas or a specified spiritual "track" that someone else prescribes. Let's together read, reflect, ruminate and respond. Let's not be afraid to have questions that lack easy answers. Let's not think God isn't big enough to handle our doubt. Let's not limit God to our confusion and misunderstandings. Let's not box Him in either. Let's just collide with Jesus and see what He will do.

We are broken. We have been abused, used, betrayed, judged, manipulated, beat down and lied to. We have skeletons in the closet, a long list of mistakes, shady pasts, paralytic fear and deep-seated bitterness we struggle with. We will not pretend we are someone we aren't, and we won't ask you to either. We are not put together. We are not perfect. We are not immortal. We are not finished, faultless or foolproof. We are not Christian poster children. We are sojourners, inviting you, in your brokenness, to walk alongside us in ours, and together, we will collide with Jesus and by His wounds, we will be made whole.

We aren't afraid to engage our brokenness or yours. We no longer want our past to determine our present. We know that the pain we have experienced can easily walk into all of our collisions and we want more than that for our lives. We want to see our wounds find their Healer. We want to see our pain experience redemption. We want to see our brokenness be used for good. We know there's no other way around pain than to allow Jesus to meet us in it. So, we let Him. We sit in discomfort, we remember, we grieve, we cry, we forgive, we get angry and cry out like the Psalmist. But we don't avoid, ignore or devalue our pain or yours. We believe God meets us where we are. We don't believe you have to get it together before God will run into your life. It is actually in the midst of pain and brokenness that God does His greatest work.

We have big hopes. We believe that this project, to create content that invites people to collide with Jesus, has the potential to change your life and your friends' lives and your neighbors and on and on. We believe this because when people collide with Jesus they are never the same. We see this all the time in our ministry. When people run into who God is, they become who they are made to be. We have big God-sized dreams that when we together, collide with Jesus, we will be changed and then we together can change the world.

How to use this study

We hand crafted this study for women just like you. It has been designed to be used in the way that works best, personally, for wherever you find yourself. We know that women experience a variety of different roles, seasons, and circumstances. We encourage you to engage this study with your morning cup o' coffee, to pull it out of your handbag while you wait for your kids to be done with soccer practice. Grab it off the shelf when you are struggling to find purpose or invite some friends over and do it together. Jesus meets you along the way, so as you journey, doing whatever it is you do, may you enjoy colliding with Him.

We fashioned this study with freedom and joy in mind. Our hope is that colliding with Jesus brings gratification and not guilt, life and not condemnation, power and not oppression. So please be a friend to yourself and enter into this study with freedom knowing God invites you to come and collide with Him, not so He can critique you or grade you, but so He can love and spend time with you. God doesn't have an expectation of the number of pages you must read or a time-line of how fast you must complete this study. God won't be mad at you if you leave some reflection questions blank or even if you think a question we ask is dumb. It probably is. God merely wants to be with you. Enjoy your time with Him.

We constructed this study with a few simple prompts to invite your engagement.

Read

We will invite you to read a passage of Scripture that unfolds a collision with Jesus and corresponding Scripture that applies. Our desire is that as you see Jesus collide with others, you will also experience this living God collide with you.

Reflect

Our hope is that you would not just read or "know facts" about the Bible, but instead that you would allow your heart and mind to go to deeper places: to reflect, to think, to mull, to consider. It is in our reflection that God can have some of His greatest conversations with each one of us. And it is in these conversations that transformation, guidance, wisdom and healing take place. We have intentionally written questions that will invite you to purposely reflect so that you can experience just that.

Ruminate

There will be points where we will encourage you to stop and chew, wrestle, learn or meditate on more. This is where ruminating on thoughts, Scripture, and quotes will bless you and invite you further into a collision with Jesus.

Respond

You can't stay the same and go with God. Every time Jesus collides with people they are forever transformed. He often calls us to take action, to pray, to move, to serve, to give, to lay down, to surrender, to not merely be "hearers" of the word but "doers". Our hope is that we will not just "study" God, but that we will become people who respond to our collisions with Jesus in a way that helps us see transformation in our own lives, that then leads to transformation in the lives of those around us.

Leader Guide

When we study God's word together, we hear multiple perspectives which help enhance our experience. If you would like to lead a group of women through this study, we have created a Leader Guide which you will find at the end of this book. Our hope is that this guide will help you lead your group into meaningful conversation as you support and encourage one another.

Let's collide . . .

THE ANXIETY EPIDEMIC

THE BIRDS & THE LILIES

For a recent birthday I got to experience what a spa called the "foot refresher." I checked in and they handed me the clipboardy thing. On it was the paperwork you have to fill out, telling them about all the bad rashes, STD's, and pregnancies you've ever had or not had in your life. I swear spas collect more information than surgeons. But anyhoo, the receptionist walked me to the "relaxation" room. She said I could "up" my service from a fifty-minute massage to an eighty-minute. I thought, "You know what? It's my birthday, I might do that." So, I asked them how much it would be and she said it would be seventy bucks. I decided to splurge with some gift money I had received.

They invited me to get all zen before the massage so I walked over to the tea bar. I picked mint. I always do unless jasmine is an option. Then I sat in my chair, fidgeting to get cozy. I had to pee, so I headed down the hall to the bathroom with no flip flops, no bra, no makeup and no brush. I looked like a million bucks. When I got back to the relaxation room, a sweet pregnant lady walked in and sat across from me. In order to avoid eye contact and not interrupt her zen time, I slanted my gaze slightly left and stared at the fireplace. Now I was socially awkward, which I don't often feel. She got up because she either felt my weird vibe or she, too, discovered the tea.

The second she got up, the door opened and in walked a man with an eye patch. I kid you not. He was probably twenty years older than me and he seemed drunk, but probably more like "relaxed." He scooted in and took the first chair he saw, which was the pregnant lady's chair. I started to feel anxious like, "Should I say something so the woman can get her seat back?" Then I reminded myself, "She's a big girl. She can probably speak up for herself."

I looked over to observe how their interaction was going to go down and you wouldn't believe it - this man's robe was popped open and he was showing ALL his man parts! I'll tell you what, if Jesus Himself would have been chilling in that spa, I'm pretty sure He would have turned water into whiiii-te underwear. So much for my relaxation. I was mortified, stunned, and anxious.

The pregnant lady walked over. Her hands were full, one with tea and the other with those healthy trail mix snacks you get at places like this with fruit that's probably been drying since 1804 and leaves you wondering where the chocolate is. I just completely passed on the offer but, apparently she was a health nut. She was so sweet as she moved back and forth, observing the scenario and trying to figure out what to do. I don't think she cared that this man took her seat, except for the fact that he was sitting on her clipboard thingy. She invited him to remain in his seat but she pointed, "My... my... my forms." He offered to move. She declined. I left to pee.

The entire massage, my mind was like a tennis match on some kind of upper. All the things I needed to do started making giant lists in my head, and I got anxious because I didn't have a pencil to write them down. I worried I would forget them. I started getting anxious about the Collide event we had coming up. How would we pull off feeding almost a thousand ladies? How would we register them? How would we show them they are loved? When would I find time to write a message? And would this be the Collide gathering where I don't have a message or it sucks and finally God reveals to everyone that I might not be cut out for this? And then I started worrying about a friendship. I wondered if we were misunderstanding each other and what the outcome would be and... I worried if my headaches mean I have a tumor? The next thing you know I was down the road of saying goodbye to my kids forever because that hypothetical tumor killed me.

The entire massage I didn't feel my feet, I felt my anxiety.

I looked up at the masseuse and apologized because I had to get up off the table and go to the bathroom again. When I returned for the rest of my massage she said, "Try to get back into your happy place." Get back into my happy place? I never got into my happy place. I walked out to pay and the lady said, "That will be $189." Apparently the $70 was not for the entire bill but for the extra few minutes. I was floored. Now I felt dumb, and I felt anxious that I felt dumb. I was trying to decide if I should complain about the communication or just pay the bill. I was kicking myself for not being hip on spa prices. I was sweating and bummed that I couldn't just go and enjoy myself without money being a thing. So I charged it and then my husband and I fought over the excessive $200 foot massage that I didn't even enjoy because instead I got massaged by worry and anxiety.

Life is like a trip to the spa where we seek to find that "happy place" but even with the best of intentions, awkwardness, confrontations, small bladders and big bills find us. And so do cancer and bankruptcy, betrayal and divorce, mental illness and learning disabilities, family dysfunction and friendship drama. Worry is so sneaky and fierce that it finds us at work, in bed, in waiting rooms, flying in airplanes, and even in spas.

We actually live in what some are calling the "Anxiety Culture". We worry as daughters, mothers and grandmothers. We're getting gray hairs because we're nervous Nellies. We're taking chill pills because we're worried sick. We're stress cases with stress balls. We have economic anxiety, political anxiety, financial anxiety, and relational anxiety. We worry about failing. We worry about succeeding. We worry about getting too much attention. We worry about not getting any attention. We worry about getting into school. We worry about getting out of school. We worry about being late. We worry about being too early. We worry about getting a date. We worry about getting out of dates. We worry about getting married and we get married and worry about getting divorced, then we worry about getting married again. We worry our dreams won't come true, and we worry that they will.

Reflect

Worry can present itself differently for each one of us. Circle below which of the following ways worry presents itself for you?

insomnia

self-medicating

stress eating

shop-aholism

busyness

doing too much to please everyone around me

pacing

sweaty palms

lack of self-care

impatience

irritability

overreacting

faster than normal heart rate

overanalyzing decisions

controlling things

lack of engagement

the inability to filter the hypothetical from reality

WORRY IS A FRIEND TO ALL, stopping by FOR VISITS ALL too often, AND FOR SOME, IT HAS ACTUALLY MOVED IN AND BECOME OUR ROOMMATE.

for some of us, one second we can be doing okay and the next a Facebook post sends us into Anxiousville. For others, anxiety looks like a nagging sense that gets in the way of our lives every single day and maybe it has for years. For some, we have sought the counsel of healthcare professionals and have come to accept that worry and anxiety might be a part of us - a thorn, if you will - that we might always have on this side of the perfect place we call Heaven. Worry is a friend to all, stopping by for visits all too often, and for some, it has actually moved in and become our roommate.

Reflect

Are you surprised by seeing the ways worry presents itself in your life on the previous page?

Do you worry on occasion, or has anxiety moved in and become your roommate?

Ruminate

Statistics are pointing to worry being an epidemic in our country. Here are some statistics on worry and anxiety that should alarm us:

- In 2002 the World Mental Health Survey found that Americans were the most anxious people in the 14 countries studied, with more clinically significant levels of anxiety than people in Nigeria, Lebanon and Ukraine.[1]

- In 2015-2016 stress accounted for 37% of all work related ill health cases[2]

- Anxiety disorders are the most common mental illness affecting Americans, costing the United States some $42 billion a year[3] and between 1997 and 2004, Americans more than doubled their spending on anti-anxiety medications.[4]

- One article said "…surveys of more than 200,000 incoming freshmen.. reported all-time lows in overall mental health and emotional stability.."[5]

- Psychologist Robert Leahy believes: "The average high school kid today has the same level of anxiety as the average psychiatric patient in the early 1950s."[6]

- Rates of stress, anxiety and depression are rising sharply among teenage girls in what mental health specialists say is a "deeply worrying" trend…that began with the rise of social media.[7]

- And women are twice as likely to suffer as men, according to the Anxiety Disorders Association of America.[8]

1 www.nytimes.com/2015/07/19/opinion/sunday/the-anxious-americans.html
2 Lucado, Max. *Anxious for Nothing: Finding Calm in a Chaotic World.* Thomas Nelson, 2017.
3 www.cnn.com/2016/06/08/health/women-anxiety-disorders/index.html
4 Lucado, Max. *Anxious for Nothing: Finding Calm in a Chaotic World.* Thomas Nelson, 2017.
5 www.slate.com/articles/arts/culturebox/2011/01/its_not_the_job_market.html
6 www.psychologytoday.com/us/blog/anxiety-files/200804/how-big-problem-is-anxiety
7 www.theguardian.com/society/2017/sep/23/stress-anxiety-fuel-mental-health-crisis-girls-young-women
8 www.nbcnews.com/id/39335628/ns/health-mental_health/t/why-are-anxiety-disorders-among-women-rise

Reflect

Which of these stats alarm you? Why?

What is all this worry and anxiety in our culture trying to tell us? If it had a voice, what would it say?

Example: Worry is telling us we don't have peace.

Fill in the blank with what we are often told as women when we exhibit anxious or stressful feelings?

You must be about to start your…_____.

Are you …___pregnant___?

You're acting …_____.

You're …___crazy___.

Don't be such a worry…_____.

You're so… ___hormonal___.

What kind of statements would be helpful to hear when you're feeling stressed?

There are many things we do to help relieve our own stress and worry. A few of them are:

- **We try to alleviate worry with happiness.** Stressed? Go to Disneyland, the happiest place on the planet. Unhappy with your life? Get a massage. Discontent about what you look like? Go to the mall and buy some new clothes.

- **We try to make worry disappear through busyness.** We work it away. We get over-involved, we try harder, we socialize like crazy, all in the hopes that our efforts will make the things we worry about dissipate.

- **We try to halt anxiety through apathy.** We stop caring because we think if we stop caring we can avoid the worry and stress that goes along with it.

- **We try to chill out with escapism.** We escape into fantasy. We drink lots of cocktails. We become addicted to trash TV. We play Candy Crush like crazy. Julian Somers, an associate professor of health sciences at Simon Fraser University in Canada, speaks to the rise in anxiety levels saying, "One important result is the overlap between anxiety and addiction. This means that treatment providers need to consider a focus on anxiety, and [it] raises the possibility that people may use substances in ways that both increase and help manage their anxiety symptoms."[9] This is interesting because in our attempt to become less anxious, we often use escapism as a way to cope, which can actually create more worry and anxiety than we had to begin with.

- **We try to say goodbye to stress by ignoring it.** We live in potentially the most anxious culture and yet we say to one another: "Don't worry about a thing." "Don't worry your pretty little head about it." "Not to worry." "Don't worry - be happy now." As if ignoring our anxiety will make it all go away.

We have all tried a lot of things to set ourselves free from worry: yoga, tea, puppies, kale, exercise, and meditation. All these are good, especially the puppies, but do they set us free? Most of us have tried to make our worry and anxiety go away with escapism, apathy, Disneyland, massage, pilates, working more, working less, drinking more coffee, drinking less coffee, inspirational memes, Netflix binging, Pinterest crafts and swiping right when maybe we should have swiped left. So often our attempts to cure our anxiety still leaves us as anxious as ever.

9 www.cnn.com/2016/06/08/health/women-anxiety-disorders/index.html

> **worry**
> *verb* wor·ry \ ‘wer-ē , ‘we-rē \
> *to choke or strangle.*

Reflect

How about your life - how would you say it is being choked or strangled by worry?

What have you personally tried to do to make your worry go away?

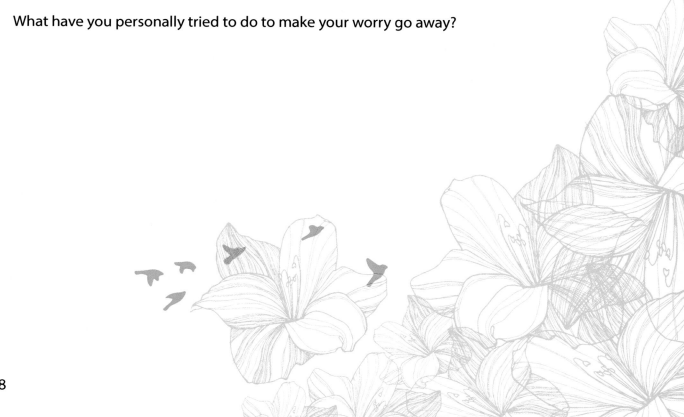

Set your watch or phone alarm and for the next 5 minutes, brain dump all that you are worried about on this page and the following page. You can write down names, work deadlines, hypothetical fears, anxious thoughts, finances, decisions needing to be made or whatever comes to your mind.

What surprised you in doing this 5-minute exercise?

Did you notice a theme regarding your worries?

Did you notice what happened the longer time went on?

What do these two pages of worry tell you?

WHAT IF THERE IS *another way?*

Respond

What if there is another way than all of this? Jesus says there is. As you find yourself desiring to be set free from the worry and fear, the anxiety and attempts to rescue yourself and those around you, let's pray this prayer. Feel free to read the prayer provided to yourself as a declaration of your hope and a request of God to enter into all that worries you and bring about His peace.

God,

You know my thoughts, You know my circumstances, You know the mess I'm in, You know the mess I've made, and the mess others have made in my life. You know where I am hurting and You know what keeps me up at night. None of these are a surprise to You. God, I ask that You come into all this. God, take my worry and replace it with peace. Take my doubt and replace it with faith. Take my fear and replace it with hope. I need You to show me another way than worry and anxiety. You are a God who comes, who enters in, who collides. Please Jesus, collide with me.

Amen.

In this Bible study, we will intentionally center around Matthew 6 where Jesus speaks into worry. We will get there, but first we will process a bit around common experiences we have due to worry and fear. Our hope is that this study will meet each one of you where you, and those you love, are at. We recognize that worry and anxiety can be experienced for a myriad of reasons and can be calmed by a multitude of helps. It is our intention to cover a diverse number of ways women feel anxious, from everyday common stressors, to material treasures, to childhood wounds, to deep seated worth issues. We are deeply aware that not all women are the same, nor are their experiences, but we can learn from each other. We do believe, without a shadow of a doubt, that God meets each one of us where we are at. So we invite you to collide with Jesus as He meets you personally and powerfully and calls you to another way than worry and anxiety - a way of peace, hope and faith.

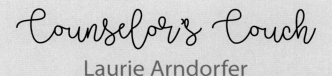

Counselor's Couch

Laurie Arndorfer

One of Collide's core values is to recognize brokenness so it can be made whole. We believe God desires for each one of us to say yes to walking towards wholeness. We have a growing community of women walking towards healing, as well as a community of counselors who are partnering with us to this end. We hope you not only enjoy hearing a counselor's voice here, but that you open yourself up to the transformational work God is personally inviting you into so that you can see His healing as a reality in your life. We want to make sure that we address, both Jesus' sermon on worry in this study, but also point people who might have an anxiety disorder to help beyond this.

Anxiety is a normal response to stress. In small increments, it can help motivate us to accomplish things and to get organized. It can also alert us to a potentially dangerous situation and activate the fight or flight response to help us to escape. So, in some ways, anxiety can be a good thing. However, some people struggle, not with mild episodes of anxiety, but with a true anxiety disorder. An anxiety disorder involves intense and excessive anxiety, along with other symptoms, which can be overwhelming and interfere with normal functioning. Some anxiety disorders include Generalized Anxiety Disorder, Panic Disorder, and Social Anxiety Disorder.

How to tell if you have normal anxiety or an anxiety disorder:

1. Is there a stressor?

Normal anxiety occurs in response to a stressor, such as an upcoming interview or other life event, a presentation, or meeting someone for the first time. In those situations, feeling a few butterflies in the stomach is completely normal. Usually when the stressor is over, the anxiety dissipates.

However, some people feel anxiety most days, but they are unable to identify a stressor that is causing it. They have trouble controlling the anxiety and it may become debilitating. They may also have physical symptoms along with the feelings of worry, including frequent muscle tension, restlessness, difficulty falling or staying asleep, frequent trips to the bathroom, fatigue, irritability and poor concentration. If these symptoms continue for a significant length of time, this may indicate that someone has Generalized Anxiety Disorder, and may need to seek help.

2. Intensity and Duration

Normal anxiety is short lived and does not lead someone to change his or her normal schedule or routines. Someone studying for an exam may be anxious the day of the exam, but someone with an anxiety disorder may be anxious and fearful about it for weeks ahead of time, then extremely anxious during the exam. Anxiety disorders can produce intense, excessive emotional responses. Panic disorder involves a sudden overwhelming tidal wave of anxiety along with symptoms such as shortness of breath, chest tightness, flushing, sweating, dizziness, feeling detached or disconnected, increased heart rate and a sense of impending doom. Though most panic attacks are brief, they occur randomly and are very intense. People then worry about having the next attack as it is unclear what brought it on in the first place.

3. Impairment

Anxiety disorders can affect someone's entire life. Severe social anxiety may impair individuals from going to events where there are crowds or people that they don't know well. Anxiety can also impair functioning at work or school. Some anxiety symptoms such as panic attacks may even lead someone to avoid their usual activities such as work or school altogether, or to even avoid spending time with people they care about. In a severe form of avoidance called agoraphobia, it may even become difficult to go to the grocery or other crowded places which trigger anxiety. Without help, individuals can get to the point where they are unable to leave the house.

If you have excessive anxiety…

Do not be afraid to ask for help if you are struggling or if any of the above scenarios apply to your life. You are not alone. There are approximately 40 million adults in the United States who have anxiety disorders. The good news is that these disorders are very treatable! Many people benefit from psychotherapy and there are also medications available that can be beneficial in treating these conditions. Take the first courageous step to manage these symptoms by contacting a local psychologist or therapist to consider counseling or a psychiatrist to discuss medication options.

Written by Laurie Arndorfer, MD

YOU SHOULD
BE AFRAID

My friend, Scott Erickson, who travels all over the world creating amazing artwork that proclaims powerful messages and invokes profound thought, said to me once, "You know what worry says? Worry says, 'You should be afraid.' "

Worry and fear have a funny relationship. They seem to play off each other. Worry tells us to fear and fear tells us to worry. When we worry that we won't be able to pay our bills, we hear, "You should be afraid you're going to lose your house." When we worry that our kids are going to get hurt by someone they care about, we hear, "You should be afraid they will be left out and have no friends. "When we Google our health symptoms, we hear, "You should be afraid because you probably have cancer."

Common, everyday worry can start to breed hypotheticals. I know for me, I can already begin writing a story in my head that has not happened but begins to feel like reality. Recently, my son found a large, painful lump near his neck and the next thing you know I was playing out how I would respond in front of my teenager to the horrible news when the doctor delivered it. Of course, hours later at his appointment, the doctor seemed certain that it was an enlarged lymph node due to his immune system fighting something. But for hours my worry created a fear that wrote a false story, that then created more anxiety and more fear. Sometimes what we fear does become our reality, but often times, it doesn't and yet we have already begun to operate out of the false hypotheticals we convinced ourselves would come true. Whether what we fear becomes a reality or it doesn't, our fear and panic do little to help (but we will talk about that more later).

Reflect

How is worry telling you to be afraid?

How would you describe the relationship between worry and fear in your life?

When is the last time your fear started writing a hypothetical story in your head?

Before we Tackle Jesus' sermon on worry and anxiety, we need to pause and reflect on what all this worry is doing. If worry is causing fear to boss us around, we need to stare it straight in the eyes. The Lord speaks to our great tendency to fear. In fact, the Bible references hundreds of passages where God tells His people not to fear. "Do not be afraid" is one of the most repeated commands in the Bible.

Reflect

When God tells you not to fear, how do you feel like responding?

○ Easy for you to say.

○ I wouldn't be so afraid if you would change my circumstances.

○ You try being me.

○ That sounds great in theory but it's hard to put into practice.

○ I'm tryyyyying.

○ You're right! I will not be afraid!

○ Other _____

Ruminate

Read the following verses where God is adamant about not letting fear overtake our lives and circle the ones that you needed to hear most today.

Do not be afraid. . . .I am your shield, your very great reward. **Genesis 15:1**

Do not be afraid. . . .for I am with you. **Genesis 26:24**

Do not be afraid. . . .for the Lord your God will be with you wherever you go. **Joshua 1:9**

Do not be afraid. . . .I have given them into your hand. Not one of them will be able to withstand you. **Joshua 10:8**

Do not be afraid. . . .You are not going to die. **Judges 6:23**

Do not be afraid. . . .of what you have heard. **2 Kings 19:6**

Do not be afraid. . . .for the battle is not yours, but God's. **2 Chronicles 20:15**

Do not be afraid. . . .the Lord will be with you. **2 Chronicles 20:17**

Do not be afraid. . . .for I myself will help you. **Isaiah 41:14**

Do not be afraid. . . .for I am with you; I will bring your children from the east and gather you from the west. **Isaiah 43:5**

Do not be afraid. . . .For I will pour water on the thirsty land. **Isaiah 44:3**

Do not be afraid. . . .Is there any God besides me? No, there is no other rock: I know not one. **Isaiah 44:8**

Do not be afraid. . . .you will not suffer shame. . .you will not be humiliated. **Isaiah 54:4**

Do not be afraid. . . .for I am with you and will rescue you. **Jeremiah 1:8**

Do not be afraid. . . .of them or their words. . .though briers and thorns are all around you. **Ezekiel 2:6**

Do not be afraid. . . .though they are a rebellious people. **Ezekiel 3:9**

Do not be afraid. . . .Since the first day that you set your mind to gain understanding and to humble yourself before God, your words were heard. **Daniel 10:12**

Do not be afraid. . . .but let your hands be strong. **Zechariah 8:13**

Do not be afraid. . . .There is nothing concealed that will not be disclosed, or hidden that will not be made known. **Matthew 10:26**

Do not be afraid. . . .of those who kill the body but cannot kill the soul. **Matthew 10:28**

Do not be afraid. . . .for your Father has been pleased to give you the kingdom. **Luke 12:32**

Do not be afraid. . . .keep on speaking, do not be silent. **Acts 18:9**

Do not be afraid. . . .I am the First and the Last. **Revelation 1:17**

Do not be afraid. . . .I will give you the crown of life. **Revelation 2:10**

(This list can be found in its entirety to be printed for use on our Resource page at wecollide.net/resources)

I think the Lord reiterates His hope that we would not fear because God knows the power that fear has over our lives. Fear paralyzes us. It bosses us around. It hinders us. It keeps us hiding. It turns us into workhorses and control freaks. It ruins relationships and it crushes dreams. Fear is a big bad force in our lives. Fear can keep us in the dark, outside of all light. Fear can squelch our faith. Fear can destroy our relationships. And over and over again throughout Scripture God tells us, "Do not be afraid." I don't think God is lacking empathy or compassion for what we have been through or what we are currently experiencing. I don't think God is being bossy or judgemental or making fun of what we fear. I think God wants to remind us who is Boss, who is bigger, who is on our side and who wins in the end.

I remember sitting in a counseling office once and the counselor sat listening to me because that's what I paid him to do. After about 35 minutes of my 60 minute time allotment of him listening to me share all my worries and fears, he looked at me and said, "You need to learn to tell yourself a different story." This wise counselor saw that so often (not always) what I worry about begins to write stories in my mind that may or may not be true, and then I begin to operate on those stories that I have told myself. He challenged me for one week, when I found myself worried or fretting to tell myself five other stories that might be true other than the one I worried about. I have to tell you, this homework assignment radically challenged me. I couldn't believe how frequently my worry was making up stories about outcomes, relationships, people's motives, and so many other things. I began to see how my fear was convincing me to prepare for the worst, to assume things about other people, and to expect bad things to happen. I don't share this with you because I'm proud of it. I share this with you because this illustrates the power of fear birthed from worry in our lives.

Reflect

When you are experiencing stress in a relationship, how often do you assume things about the other person?

Think of a current circumstance that is causing you anxiety. What story are you telling yourself that may or may not be true?

Take a moment to practice telling yourself 5 different stories in place of the one you are telling yourself currently. (For example, when you are in a circumstance where a friend is not returning your calls and you have yourself convinced she is distancing herself from you, a new story may be to tell yourself: my friend is very busy and has a lot going on with her family right now.)

Do you think fear holds power over your life in any way and if so, how?

What do you love about a God who doesn't want fear to dominate our lives?

We see God's desire to alleviate our fear and worry over and over again in collisions with Jesus. The man waiting by the waters in the hopes they would heal him, was worried sick that he would never make it down to the place that promised healing. And it was Jesus who came to him and freed him from his fear and relieved him of his paralysis.

It was Martha who was walking around with a bee in her bonnet trying to be the hostess with the mostest, fretting about this, that and the other thing and it was Jesus who showed up to free her from a life that was upset about many things. It was Jesus who showed up at just the right time to free the woman who had been caught sleeping with someone other than her husband and she was about to undergo the standard, expected punishment for such action. This woman was frightened for her life and Jesus came to give her freedom. He freed her despite the mess she made, and despite the mess freeing her would make for Him with the religious Pharisees who would then set out to kill him.

After freeing the adulteress, Jesus goes onto say in **John 8:36** *"So if the Son sets you free, you will be free indeed."* Jesus is in the business of freeing people. I love that we have a God who collides with us and when He does, His number one priority is not to get us to learn our lessons or memorize His commands, nor is it to protect Himself. Instead, high on God's priority list seems to be freeing us.

GOD WANTS FOR US *freedom, not fear.*

Ruminate

Read the passages below and write beneath an action that you can take to walk toward freedom and away from fear:

○ *I will walk about in freedom, for I have sought out your precepts.* **Psalm 119:45**

seek His precepts

○ *Now the Lord is the Spirit, and where the Spirit of the Lord is, there is freedom.* **2 Corinthians 3:17**

○ *It is for freedom that Christ has set us free. Stand firm, then, and do not let yourselves be burdened again by a yoke of slavery.* **Galatians 5:1**

○ *In him and through faith in him we may approach God with freedom and confidence.* **Ephesians 3:12**

○ *But whoever looks intently into the perfect law that gives freedom, and continues in it—not forgetting what they have heard, but doing it—they will be blessed in what they do.* **James 1:25**

○ *Speak and act as those who are going to be judged by the law that gives freedom.* **James 2:12**

○ *Live as free people, but do not use your freedom as a cover-up for evil; live as God's slaves.* **1 Peter 2:16**

God desires for us, freedom. So if worry is breeding fear and fear is holding your life back, it's time to take note and to take action. As we move into Jesus' life-changing message on worry, please be paying attention to how anxiety and fear have a relationship with each other in your life. Note how often you are reacting to what worry born fear is telling you to do. American novelist, Ralph Ellison said "When I discover who I am, I'll be free."[10] Self awareness is often the beginning of change. Jesus helps us see who we are so that we can transform into who we are meant to be. We see this when Jesus collided with the woman at the well and helped her see who she had become. When He

Jesus is in the business of freeing people.

36

10 Ellison, Ralph. *The Invisible Man. 2nd ed.,* Vintage Books, 1995.

laid out the pattern in her life that was not working, she saw who she had become and that was the beginning of her leaving her old life and trading it in for her new one. The beginning of winning the battle on worry and fear is recognizing first how badly we might be losing it. We have to be women who begin to see how worry births fear and fear bosses us around and we begin to be its puppet. When we discover our patterns, our reactions and the root of why we worry, we will also discover freedom.

I just love the song, "His Eye Is on The Sparrow." (If you haven't heard it, I recommend checking out the late, great Whitney Houston version on YouTube). Civilla Martin, who wrote this song, and her husband developed a deep friendship with a couple by the name of Mr. and Mrs. Doolittle. Mrs. Doolittle had been bedridden for almost twenty years and her husband was handicapped and in a wheelchair. Despite their hardship, they lived inspiring Christian lives. One day Civilla and her husband asked what the Doolittle's secret was. Mrs. Doolittle quite simply said: "His eye is on the sparrow, and I know He watches me."[11] Her words inspired the gorgeous hymn whose lyrics say:

"Whenever I am *tempted,* whenever *clouds arise,* when songs give place to *sighing,* when *hope* within me dies, draw the *closer* to Him, from care He *sets me free,* His eye is on the *sparrow,* and I *know* He watches me…"

How does God set us free? Civilla Martin was right... from care. When we fully grasp the care, value and love God places on us, our worry begins to decrease and our freedom begins to increase. I love that. We will see this as we journey together. As we process the ways worry and fear have us tied up, strangled and enslaved, may we allow God's care to meet us and set us free.

"WHEN I DISCOVER WHO I AM, I'LL BE FREE." RALPH ELLISON

Respond

Feel free to write your own hymn by adding your own words to the one below or refer back to the original hymn on p. 37 and add in Civilla Martin's lyrics. Pray this hymn out loud as a yearning for the Son to set you free, trusting, that's what He is in the business of doing.

Lord,

Whenever I am _____

whenever _____ arises

When _____ give place to sighing

When _____ within me dies

I draw the closer to You,

from care You set me free;

Your eye is on the sparrow

and I know You watch me.

Amen

Your Story

Kristen

We encourage women to bravely and authentically tell their stories as they really are. We hope this "your story" meets you in yours.

Fear was an unwanted presence that dominated my experience for twenty years. It would come and go, sometimes arriving on the scene as a quiet voice in the back of my head or rearing its head like a loud, thundering voice that threatened to overcome me.

I struggled with anxiety and Obsessive Compulsive Disorder (OCD). In case you're not familiar with what OCD means, here is a definition: Obsessions are intrusive, unwanted thoughts that trigger anxiety, distress and uncertainty. Compulsions are learned behaviours, which become repetitive and habitual when they are associated with relief from anxiety.

It's not an ideal way to live life, but it was my reality. Apart from the constant static of fear in my mind, the time it took to make sure none of the bad stuff happened, through my compulsive behavior, was exhausting.

My OCD stayed with me from my childhood up until college. It was 100% exhausting, both mentally and physically. On top of that, it was isolating because I always felt like I was the only one who struggled with it and I was too scared to ask around to find community to lean on. At the end of the day, the whole experience of anxiety weighs on you: the racing thoughts, the constant stomach ache, the inability to rest, the exhaustion, the loneliness; the list could go on.

I honestly believed I would never experience the rest I knew existed on the other side of anxiety. I envied people who could walk through the day without any worries. I remember craving a break from it all, but holding a tight grip on anxiety in my efforts to make sure none of the bad stuff I was scared of actually happened. It felt unbearable. I assumed nothing would ever shift for me - until one morning.

I got desperate for something I knew could only come from pressing into the presence of God. I had heard about it and read about it, but never made the connection between my head and heart until one random, routine Monday morning drive to class.

For the first time, my mind finally got a taste of what the scriptures refer to as the "renewing of our minds" as I began to declare the peace of God over my thoughts. I began to dedicate my 20-minute drive to school every day as a time of prayer, opening up to God about what I was scared about, no matter how silly it felt. I realized I didn't have to hold anything back and as I brought to mind Jesus' words from Matthew 11:28, I was released from the burden of dealing with life alone.

I started memorizing Bible verses about peace to rewire my brain with the word of God— Romans 8:15 reminded me I'm no longer a slave to fear and gave me authority over my thoughts. I made sure to incorporate worship songs into the start of my day to help me center. All this helped me refocus my nervous energy and I found that getting into HIS PRESENCE allowed a sound mind to become a reality in my life.

I've always loved sermons, books or articles on anxiety because I wanted healing quick and fast. I was constantly searching for three easy steps to peace. But, for me, healing was a tough fight over many years that ended in chains being broken and a life of peace. It was a combination of Jesus, trusted council, community I could relate to and rewiring my brain with scripture and prayer that propelled me in the opposite direction of fear.

I'm not who I used to be. You can ask any of my family members. They've asked me before, "How is it that you are who you are now, when we remember who you used to be?" It's incredible that this transformation started with simple steps of getting into His presence.

I don't want to over glamorize my story of healing, because, like I said before, it was a tough fight. God did miraculously set me free for about four years, but then, my anxiety came back like a ton of bricks. By that point though, I had the tools to navigate anxiety so it doesn't take me down like it used to.

For many years, I had one goal that centered around erasing pieces of my story in an attempt to look strong and fearless. At the time, I didn't realize that everything I kept hidden prevented me from being utilized by God to encourage others. By not being authentic with my story, I was unable to fully walk into the spheres of strength and freedom I longed for.

I started owning my story and sharing it with confidence because I saw the way my honesty allowed other people to be honest about their struggle and in turn step towards peace and healing. I love the opportunities God has given me to encourage other people through my experience and breakthrough. My mission is to tell people that they are not alone in the midst of fear and to provide hope that there is peace on the other side of anxiety. That's what it's all about. My prayer is that my story reminds you, lovely one, that you ARE ANOINTED with a peace that gives you authority to thrive as a warrior and not a worrier.

Written by Kristen Mattila

TAKING MATTERS INTO YOUR OWN HANDS

When my friend Scott so profoundly said, "You know what worry says? Worry says, 'You should be afraid,'" my response was, "Yes, and when we are afraid, we take matters into our own hands." When we are worried about our kids, we say to ourselves, "I need to make everything better." When we're worried about getting that promotion, we work ridiculous hours. When we're worried about gaining weight, we count calories obsessively. When we're worried about being alone, we date everyone this side of Timbuktu. When we're worried about the state of our country, we binge on CNN news. When we're worried that our life feels like it's spinning out of control, we grasp for control.

How do you take matters into your own hands?

Take your hand, place it palm down in the space provided and trace it. Write words in the center that depict how you take matters into your own hands in an attempt to make things better. (Example: try too hard, overinvolved, tell people what they want to hear, bail people out, always host, etc.)

When we take matters into our own hands, we attempt to be our own rescuer and the savior of others, which only increases our need for more rescuing and saving. This is what causes broken relationships, shingles, sleepless nights, headaches, obsessions, high blood pressure, strokes, sickness, low immunity, teeth grinding, adult onset acne, stomach aches, anger, and more. Our attempts to take matters into our own hands can often create more circumstances to worry about than we had in the first place.

Reflect

List below the other stressors and worries you help create by taking matters into your own hands. For example: When I try to people please, I end up over committing to too many things and letting people down.

Do you see this to be true in other people's lives? When you think of people you care about who are taking matters into their own hands and creating more to worry about, what would you want to say to them, if you could be completely honest?

When God sees you taking matters into your own hands, trying to be your own rescuer and in turn, creating for yourself more reasons to be stressed, what do you think He would want to say to you if you were to allow Him to be completely honest?

OUR ATTEMPTS TO TAKE MATTERS INTO OUR OWN HANDS CAN OFTEN CREATE MORE CIRCUMSTANCES TO WORRY ABOUT THAN WE HAD IN THE FIRST PLACE.

FOR HE HAS *rescued us* FROM THE DOMINION OF DARKNESS AND BROUGHT US INTO THE KINGDOM OF THE SON HE LOVES.

COLOSSIANS 1:13

Ruminate

Look up the following Scriptures and write down what God has or will rescue His people from. Then, circle which ones most encourage you:

2 Samuel 22:18

Psalm 55:18

Isaiah 19:20

Jeremiah 20:13

Galatians 1:3-5

Colossians 1:13

1 Thessalonians 1:9-10

Over and over again, we see in Scripture that God reveals himself to be a Rescuer. In fact, the name Christ means "God saves". People are often named after something meaningful and significant. God's nickname should be "Rescuer." Jesus' life and death would show itself to be for that very purpose. And yet, what are we always trying to do? Rescue ourselves. We rescue ourselves from our own pain with self medication. We rescue ourselves from having to save face by hiding our mess-ups. We rescue ourselves from having to say sorry by blaming. We rescue ourselves from having to suffer by living in bubbles. We rescue ourselves from commitment by flying under the radar. We rescue ourselves from getting hurt by not getting close. We are the queens of self rescue.

GOD'S *nickname* SHOULD BE "*Rescuer.*"

I see us rescuing ourselves all the time, and it plays out in big and small ways. You know that friend of yours that so wants to please everyone around them that all their attempts to do so actually causes them to overstress, overtry, overshare, overspend and overwork? Sometimes worry begets worry. Fret begets fret. Stress begets stress. So often our attempts to rescue ourselves only create more and more to worry about. What a downward spiral!

Imagine a woman who wants to be loved, chosen, and wanted. So what does she do? She plans a lovely dinner party and invites all the women she hopes to grow in friendship with over for a soirée of sorts. She spends more than she has buying flowers and napkins and prawns and mousse and... presents for every guest. She wakes up early and yells at her kids for leaving things around the house, demanding they help set up for the party too. She makes such fancy plans that she is now biting her family's heads off because she's so stressed out and still has to fold the white napkins into the shape of some flying bird

she saw on Pinterest. She also still has to pick flowers in her garden and iron the table cloths. She still has to argue with her husband over how much she spent on all this. She still has to marinate the steak and wrap the boxes and write the place cards. This woman is stressed out because she wants everything to be "just so". Just so… she will feel loved and valued.

Her deepest desire leads to her greatest anxiety which leads to her biggest fear… which is that none of these guests will love, value and choose her. So she does everything to take matters into her own hands and doing that seems to create more worry, more stress, more heartache. It creates marital spats, financial stress, and mom guilt. How often are we like her?

It amazes me that we even attempt to rescue ourselves in such ordinary, common, everyday ways that can be masked as "normal" or seen as "small." I certainly find myself taking matters into my own hands in ways that I might not even realize or ways that you might not even see. And maybe you do too. I try to come to my own aid in deeper, darker and devastatingly more anxious ways than fancy dinner parties. But my point in using such a "first world problem" example, is that even in something seemingly Pinnable, I am trying to relieve my own pain, fear and worry. And in doing so, I often actually cause more of it.

Reflect

Label what you think this party planner extraordinaire woman's deepest desire, greatest anxiety and biggest fear in this circumstance is. What do you want to say to this woman in response to each?

Her deepest desire: _____to be loved and chosen_____

Your response: Friend you shouldn't have to impress people for them to love you - they should love you as you are, no white table cloths and all

Her greatest anxiety: _____things won't go as planned_____

Your response:

Her biggest fear: _none of the guests will love, value and choose her_

Your response:

What about yours, and your current circumstance? What do you want to say to yourself in response to:

Your deepest desire: _____

Your response:

Your greatest anxiety: _____

Your response:

Your biggest fear: _____

Your response:

I WILL TAKE all you've got IN YOUR HANDS into Mine.

I can be like this girl. And maybe you can too. So often my stress and worry can come from my own making. I often manufacture my own reasons to be anxious because I am trying too hard, working too much, trying to rescue everyone around me and attempting to look successful even when I'm failing. All of our attempts to take matters into our own hands rip control, trust, help and provision right out of God's. I think if God were to show up in the flesh in my kitchen, when I'm trying to make everything Instagram perfect so people will like me because they liked my party, God might have something to say. I think God would want to say, "Whatever it is that you desire, that is causing your anxiety, that is your biggest fear, let me take that into My hands. Let me be your Help, your Provision and your Rescuer." I think God would take over my party planning, people pleasing, problem solving, panic mode self. I think He would set down the napkins, set down the garden shears, set down the iron, and set down me. And I think He would say, "I will take all you've got in your hands into Mine. Let me be your Rescuer."

Respond

Pray to the One whose very name means, God saves.

Christ,

I need You to save me from trying to save myself. I've spent moments my whole life trying to do that and I'm tired. Thank you God that You are a God whose entire mission is about saving me because I can't seem to save myself. You know all the ways my life needs rescue and all the ways I am trying to rescue my own desires, anxiety and fear. I pray that You would come to my Aid. Be my Help. Please take matters out of my hands and take them into Yours. I want to trust You to be my Rescuer. I am handing over the job I've assumed for far too long and I am giving it to You. You are way more qualified to be called Rescuer than I am. Christ, collide with me in all ways my life is crying out for rescue.

Amen

Counselor's Couch
Steve Call

Worry is often our body's way of trying to protect and even prepare us. Our worry is an attempt to prepare us for the known and the unknown. Sometimes worry is actually our body's way of talking to us. Our worry is a form of communication and it might be helpful to listen to it. Listen to what it is trying to say. Sometimes when we attempt to ignore or dismiss it, it becomes louder. Similar to a young infant who has a need, if we ignore the need, he/she becomes louder. So, let's perhaps think about worry as an attempt to communicate something. And for many of us, the worry is an attempt to communicate fear. Rather than rescue ourselves from the fear and worry, we can be encouraged to listen to it. It has something to say that is worth being heard.

Let's listen to what the worry is attempting to communicate. So, initially my worry might be something like, "I'm worried my daughter will not make any friends in her new school." One of the most helpful strategies in coping with worry/fear is to actually name it in His presence or in the presence of a trusted friend. When we name worry/fear, it actually helps us cope with it. It might be helpful to ask ourselves, "I wonder what my worry is attempting to communicate? Perhaps it is connected to fear. What am I afraid of?" When we name our fear, the intensity and preoccupation of worry lessens.

Another response to our body's worry and fear is the need for soothing. Think of the child who is worried or afraid of the dark. It's not helpful to tell that child, "There is no reason to be afraid, "or "There's no reason to worry." When the worry/fear is dismissed or minimized, the worry/fear actually intensifies. A child worried about the dark is actually able to cope with the fear and worry by the reassurance the adult offers. "Yes, of course the dark is sometimes scary. I'm here though." It is a reminder to ourselves that when we experience worry/fear, we can hear His voice, "Yes of course the dark is sometimes scary and you are worried and afraid. But I am here with you." Our worry/fear doesn't need to be rescued, it just needs to be listened to. If we take the child out of the room (rescue), it only reinforces the worry/fear for the child. So, we help children cope with the fear and worry rather than rescue them from it.

Name the fear/worry. When we name or speak the fear/worry, it actually helps soothe us. A child simply feels better when the adult listens and is attuned to the fear/worry rather than rescue the child from it. Rescue reinforces. Naming soothes. We actually feel better when we name the worry/fear in His presence and/or in the presence of another trusted adult.

Written by Steve Call PhD, MFT

52

WHAT DO YOU TREASURE?

¹⁹ "Do not lay up for yourselves treasures on earth, where moth and rust destroy and where thieves break in and steal, ²⁰ but lay up for yourselves treasures in heaven, where neither moth nor rust destroys and where thieves do not break in and steal. ²¹ For where your treasure is, there your heart will be also. ²² The eye is the lamp of the body. So, if your eye is healthy, your whole body will be full of light, ²³ but if your eye is bad, your whole body will be full of darkness. If then the light in you is darkness, how great is the darkness! ²⁴ No one can serve two masters, for either he will hate the one and love the other, or he will be devoted to the one and despise the other. You cannot serve God and money. ²⁵ Therefore I tell you, do not be anxious about your life, what you will eat or what you will drink, nor about your body, what you will put on. Is not life more than food, and the body more than clothing? ²⁶ Look at the birds of the air: they neither sow nor reap nor gather into barns, and yet your heavenly Father feeds them. Are you not of more value than they? ²⁷ And which of you by being anxious can add a single hour to his span of life? ²⁸ And why are you anxious about clothing? Consider the lilies of the field, how they grow: they neither toil nor spin, ²⁹ yet I tell you, even Solomon in all his glory was not arrayed like one of these. But if God so clothes the grass of the field, which today is alive and tomorrow is thrown into the oven, will he not much more clothe you, O you of little faith? ³¹ Therefore do not be anxious, saying, 'What shall we eat?' or 'What shall we drink?' or 'What shall we wear?' ³² For the Gentiles seek after all these things, and your heavenly Father knows that you need them all. ³³ But seek first the kingdom of God and his righteousness, and all these things will be added to you. ³⁴ Therefore do not be anxious about tomorrow, for tomorrow will be anxious for itself. Sufficient for the day is its own trouble." **Matthew 6:19-34 (ESV)**

It's fascinating that the God who made us, He actually put on flesh and blood, skull and brain, a heart and the ability to feel indigestion, anger, and emotion. Then He moved into this place with quirky, dirty, anxious people that cause anxiousness in one other. This God could not watch worry strangle our lives and not suggest another way, and so He spoke into it in His most famous sermon.

Jesus begins His thoughts on worry with some challenging points to consider and for some of us they might be hard to hear. I think it might be good to give you an upfront, honest forewarning. I promise He meets us with as much grace and gentleness as He does truth. So as you lean into His suggestions, know that He is getting somewhere with us. He comes out of the gate on worry with a heated message that is sure to challenge. So be patient and trust His love.

Jesus starts by saying, *"Do not lay up for yourselves treasures on earth, where moth and rust destroy, and where thieves **break in and steal**."* **Matthew 6:19 (ESV)**

To "break in" is literally to "dig through." It is a reference to the Palestinian home where a thief would have to chisel through the wall to get into a house.[14] The Greeks called burglars "mud-diggers" because they would have to dig into mud walls to steal other people's treasures. Jesus suggests we ought not gather up things that "mud diggers" can take from us. We store up treasures that are *perishable*; they rot, they rust, and they burn. Often what we gather can be taken from us.

Jesus suggests instead, *"lay up for yourselves treasures in heaven, where neither moth nor rust destroys, and where thieves do not **break in and steal**."* **Matthew 6:20 (ESV)** Jesus shares His divine wisdom by giving us some great advice suggesting we should store up treasures that are *imperishable*; they do not rot, they do not rust, and they do not burn.

Reflect

What do you have stored up that "mud diggers" can take from you?

14 Newman, B. M., & Stine, P. C. (1992). *A handbook on the Gospel of Matthew.* UBS Handbook Series (178). New York: United Bible Societies.

What are the things you have on your "wishlist" that you are hoping to collect soon and add to all that you already have "stored" up?

wishlist

beach house
new couch
Kitchenaid mixer

How does our culture encourage us to store up these kinds of treasures and wish for more and more?

MAYBE OUR *greatest wish* SHOULD BE IN ACQUIRING THINGS THAT CANNOT BE *taken* FROM US.

What do you store up that is imperishable and can't be taken from you?

Knowing Jesus tells us not to store up treasures that are perishable, why do you think you and I, and all our friends, have the propensity to keep storing them up anyway?

Jesus goes on to say, "For where your treasure is, there your heart will be also." **Matthew 16:21 (ESV)**

Why would Jesus bring up treasure when He is preaching on worry? Jesus suggests several reasons why we worry in Matthew 6, and what we treasure is one of them. What we worry about often points to what we treasure. If we didn't treasure it, we wouldn't worry about it. Maybe <u>some</u> of our anxiety has to do with treasuring the wrong things. Notice the word "some" is underlined. Not all of our worry is because we're treasuring the wrong things, but perhaps some. Maybe we cause some of our own anxiety. It's most definitely worth asking ourselves if Jesus is on to something.

Reflect

Do you think any of your worry and anxiety is caused by what you treasure?

Jesus continues His challenging sermon on worry, [22] *"The eye is the lamp of the body. So, if your eye is healthy, your whole body will be full of light.* [23] *But if your eye is bad, your whole body will be full of darkness. If then the light in you is darkness, how great is the darkness!"* **Matthew 6:22-23 (ESV)**

According to one commentary, "A 'bad' eye in that culture could mean either a diseased one or a stingy one...Such eyes become a symbol for the worthlessness of a stingy person."[15] He suggests that if you are generous, your life will illuminate. If you are stingy, your life will be full of darkness.

Jesus asks questions without directly asking them. Let's directly ask and answer them.

15 Keener, C. S. (1993). The IVP Bible background commentary: New Testament (Mt 6:22–23). Downers Grove, IL: InterVarsity Press.

We worry ABOUT WHAT *We Treasure.*

Reflect

When is the last time you caught yourself being generous? What were you generous with, and what inspired you to be so?

When is the last time you caught yourself being stingy? What were you being stingy with and why do you think you wanted to keep it for yourself?

Jesus connects your "eye" to the degree to which you shine light. If your "eye" is stingy, you won't illuminate and if your "eye" is generous, you will shine for all to see. What kind of "eye" would you say you have a stingy one or a generous one?

Maybe being self aware about our true level of generosity will help point us to what we treasure. And what we treasure will help guide us towards why we sometimes worry. Jesus continues to challenge what we treasure, *"No one can serve two masters: for either he will hate the one and love the other, or he will be devoted to the one and despise the other. You cannot serve God and money."* **Matthew 6:24 (ESV)**

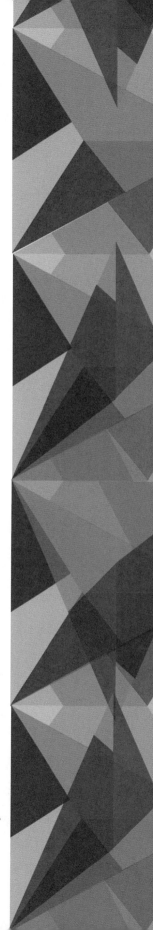

Ruminate

According to commentator C. Blomberg, "Money is more literally mammon, referring to all of a person's material resources."[16] According to the Lexham Bible Dictionary, the word money here is the word "mammon" whose meanings include: wealth, money, riches or even property.[17]

How do you think people serve wealth?

Money?

Riches?

Property?

Resources?

Circle above any that you think you sometimes serve.

"Hate" and "love" in Jewish thought were like to "choose" and "not choose."[18] Go back to **Matthew 6:24** on the previous page and substitute the word "hate" with the words "not choose" and substitute the word "love" with the word "choose." Jesus assures us we will always be forced to choose mammon over God, or God over mammon. We try to choose both, but Jesus seems to think there is no way to pull this off successfully.

16 Blomberg, C. (1992). Matthew (Vol. 22, p. 124). Nashville: Broadman & Holman Publishers.

17 Major Contributors and Editors. (2016). Mammon. In J. D. Barry, D. Bomar, D. R. Brown, R. Klippenstein, D. Mangum, C. Sinclair Wolcott, . . . W. Widder (Eds.), The Lexham Bible Dictionary. Bellingham, WA: Lexham Press.

18 Blomberg, C. (1992). Vol. 22: Matthew. The New American Commentary (124). Nashville: Broadman & Holman Publishers.

Reflect

How do you regularly face having to choose God or materials you treasure?

When we treasure God and also treasure something else, Jesus suggests we will end up being devoted to one and despising the other. Jesus seems to think in His divine wisdom that you can't serve what you put your trust in and God too. How does what you serve, steal and capture your heart away from God and cause you to despise Him?

Let's try asking a second question to help us be honest with ourselves so we can actually answer the first question… How do you know if you despise a human?

What are good questions one could ask to be able to determine if something is causing you to despise God?

Do you think you despise God?

If any of the boxes resonate with you in regards to despising God, check them:

○ You feel like you don't despise God.

○ You roll your eyes at God, like, "Really? That's what you ask of me?"

○ You think "I'll treasure what I darn well please."

○ You feel annoyed when God asks you to give something up or away.

○ You ignore God's suggestions for your life and pretend you never heard them.

○ You know what you ought to do but you do what you want to do instead.

○ You think of spending time with God as a nuisance.

○ You push God away so you don't have to serve or trust Him solely.

○ You read Scripture like this passage in Matthew and act as though it doesn't apply to you because Jesus feels like He is raining down on your parade.

I know reflecting on our treasures, our generosity levels, and who we actually serve seems pretty heavy for Jesus to start with right out of the gate. But this is where He starts, so we will start there too. Sometimes we have to get real, to get right. What I mean is… we are living with great anxiety and worry and yet we desire another way. Maybe Jesus starts here with us because He knows that we have to start with what's getting in the way before we can experience another way.

We have to allow God to meet us here and trust that He is wise and He is good and He knows what is best for our lives. And so sometimes that looks like letting Him into the hard places and being willing to be real about it. Nobody wants to say, "God, I don't trust you." Nobody wants to say, "God, I like money more than you." Nobody wants to say, "I'd rather worry than give up what I treasure." But if we can start with honesty, God can move in and bring peace into the places that are overcome by worry!

WE HAVE TO start with what's getting in the way before we can experience another way.

Respond

God,

I come to You. I am tired and weary. I am fretting and often feel overcome by stress and worry, to-dos and fear. I bring to You all that I worry about and all that I treasure. Re-prioritize me. Help me to treasure the things that You do. Help me to store up that which cannot be taken, lost or devalued. God help me to not treasure that which heaps more stress on me. Help me to everyday choose You. I will trust Your wisdom and lean into Your teaching. Lord, move out of the way anything that keeps me from experiencing Your way - the way of peace and joy.

Amen

LOOK AT
THE BIRDS

Read

[25]"Therefore I tell you, do not be anxious about your life, what you will eat or what you will drink, nor about your body, what you will put on. Is not life more than food, and the body more than clothing? [26] Look at the birds of the air; they neither sow nor reap nor gather into barns, and yet your heavenly Father feeds them. Are you not of more value than they? [27] And which of you by being anxious can add a single hour to his span of life?" **Matthew 6:25-27 (ESV)**

Reflect

When Jesus says, "Don't worry," I think we often go the place of assuming He means something He doesn't. Check the boxes that describe what you hear when someone says to you the phrase, "Don't worry!"

- ◯ Get over it.
- ◯ The things I worry about aren't important.
- ◯ Don't do anything, just wait on God.
- ◯ I'm dumb for stressing out.
- ◯ I shouldn't tell other people what I'm worried about because they just dismiss my concerns.
- ◯ I don't have enough faith.

When Jesus says, "Do not worry" He means something much different than we often hear when others use this same phrase. Jesus isn't saying, "Be lackadaisical. Don't plan for the future or work hard. Be careless about your bills. Pay no attention to the relational issues around you. Say 'whatevs' about war and politics and the current turmoil of our world."

William Barclay suggests that Jesus' teaching here aligned with the rabbis of His time. "The Jews themselves were very familiar with this attitude to life. It was the teaching of the great rabbis that a man ought to meet life with a combination of prudence and serenity. They insisted, for instance, that every man must teach his son a trade, for, they said, not to teach him a trade was to teach him to steal. That is to say, they believed in taking all the necessary steps for the prudent handling of life. But at the same time, they said, "He who has a loaf in his basket, and who says, 'What will I eat tomorrow?' is a man of little faith.'" [19] Not worrying ought to come with "prudence and serenity," not one or the other, but both.

I love what Barclay says…

"It is not *ordinary,*
prudent *foresight,*
such as *becomes* a man,
that Jesus *forbids*; it is *worry*.
Jesus is not *advocating* a shiftless,
thriftless, *reckless*, thoughtless,
improvident *attitude* to life;
he is *forbidding* a care-worn,
worried fear,
which takes *all* the
joy out of *life*." [20]

19 Barclay, W. (Ed.). (1976). The Gospel of Matthew (Vol. 1, p. 256). Philadelphia, PA: The Westminster John Knox Press.
20 Barclay, W. (Ed.). (1976). The Gospel of Matthew (Vol. 1, p. 255). Philadelphia, PA: The Westminster John Knox Press.

This is where some of us are at. We are "care-worn," worried with fear, and the joy is being sucked out of our lives. Jesus is not discouraging hard work, being smart, and preparing for what's ahead, but He is encouraging something else. I love that we have a God who cares so much about us not living a tired, worn out, exhausting worry-full life that He makes sure to meet us here and preach His heart out because this is not where He wants us to stay.

And while preaching, He says, *26 "Look at the the birds of the air; they neither sow nor reap nor gather into barns, and yet your heavenly Father feeds them. Are you not of more value than they? 27 And which of you by being anxious can add a single hour to his span of life?"* **Matthew 6:26-27 (ESV)**

Jesus shifts us from looking at all these worries to looking at the birds. What is He doing here? My friend Michelle joked after reading this, "Did Jesus join the Audubon Society?" It feels like Jesus got sucked in at REI, bought a Patagonia coat and a hammock and now He's inviting us to join Him on a nature hike. But that's not the case. Jesus is pointing to something we can look at on the daily that will remind us of what is true when our worry begins to lie. Even birds rely on God without worrying. They don't get degrees, have resumes or work their way up the corporate ladder. They don't have pantries, gardens or Costco memberships. Birds rely on

God for what they need. And what they need, He provides. When we look at the birds, we are reminded that God sustains the world around us. I wonder if when we look at a bird, it is like God reminding us…

Instead of looking at *what you worry about,* look around.

Can't you *see* that *I will take care of you?*

Look at what I *sustain.*

I support *the moon* and *the stars.*

I hold the *Earth* on its axis.

I bear up the seasons in their times.

I make the apple tree *put forth fruit*

and the carrots pop out of the ground.

I make the groundhog push its way out of the dirt

and the bear go into hibernation.

I sustain these, can I not sustain you?

Ruminate

Read this portion of **Psalm 104** which echoes Jesus' point that God sustains us. Then answer the question below.

¹⁰He makes springs pour water into the ravines; it flows between the mountains. ¹¹They give water to all the beasts of the field, the wild donkeys quench their thirst. ¹²The birds of the sky nest by the waters; they sing among the branches. ¹³He waters the mountains from his upper chambers; the land is satisfied by the fruit of his work. ¹⁴He makes grass grow for the cattle, and plants for people to cultivate—bringing forth food from the earth, ¹⁵wine that gladdens human hearts, oil to make their faces shine,and bread that sustains their hearts. ¹⁶The trees of the Lord are well watered, the cedars of Lebanon that he planted. ¹⁷There the birds make their nests; the stork has its home in the junipers. ¹⁸The high mountains belong to the wild goats; the crags are a refuge for the hyrax. ¹⁹He made the moon to mark the seasons, and the sun knows when to go down. ²⁰You bring darkness, it becomes night, and all the beasts of the forest prowl. ²¹The lions roar for their prey and seek their food from God. ²²The sun rises, and they steal away; they return and lie down in their dens. ²³Then people go out to their work, to their labor until evening...²⁷ All creatures look to you (God) to give them their food at the proper time. ²⁸When you give it to them, they gather it up; when you open your hand, they are satisfied with good things. **Psalm 104:10-23, 27-28**

Read verse 28 again. When God "opens" His hand, what does Scripture say happens?

When God opens His hand, we are satisfied with good things: sunshine on the beach, labradoodles, a promising rainbow, a powerful waterfall after a long hike, and a good glass of rosé that couldn't have been possible without the provision of God's good grapevines. God sustains all things and all satisfaction comes from His Hand. Good things are all around us, even when we are surrounded by some not so great things. I love what **James 1:17** says, *"Every good and perfect gift is from above, coming down from the Father of the heavenly lights, who does not change like shifting shadows."*

EVERY *good* AND *perfect gift* IS FROM ABOVE...
JAMES 1:17

Psalm 104:27 says, *"All creatures look to you (God) to give them their food at the proper time."* If all creatures look to God to give them what they need, why would we be any different? The Heavenly Father feeds the birds, the cattle, the plants and the wild goats. He will feed us too. But do we actually believe that? I think there are moments when it's easy to sit in creation and believe there is a Creator. When you are watching a sunset and a bluebird lands on the park bench next to you, you might be able to sense something Bigger than yourself even looking at something so small. But can you believe there's a Creator who takes care of those same birds that will also take care of you when you sit on that same park bench worried like crazy about your kids, your bills and your future? Trusting we have a God who will provide, sustain, take care of, and hold us up is challenged daily by all that worries us.

Reflect

We see that God gives the birds what they need, but why do we not trust the same for ourselves?

Think about things you have seen around you in creation, in the last week, that point to a God who is sustaining our world, earth, animals, plants and people. What have you personally seen that points to a Sustainer?

What are you most worried that God won't sustain?

Look at your hands. No really, look at them. Your hand has 27 bones, 29 joints and at least 123 named ligaments. Our opposable thumbs are what set us apart from other animals, except for the koala bear. Apparently you cannot get a tan on your palm no matter what beautiful shade of color your skin is. Your fingerprint is 100% unique. No other person in all the world has a similar fingerprint as you. Think about what human hands can do. They can play the harp, knead bread, shake on a deal, paint the Mona Lisa, hug, write love letters, start fires, sculpt pottery, build the Eiffel tower, throw a Super Bowl touchdown, and perform heart surgery. Just your hands point to a God who intricately made you.

Reflect

Go back to your hand drawing on page 44 and ponder how intricately you have been made by looking at your own hands. Write truths that you can infer knowing God made you over the top in big writing. (Example: I am unique. I am unlike any other. etc.)

JUST YOUR HANDS *point to a God* WHO INTRICATELY MADE YOU.

73

If God intricately made you, is He also able to care for you? Why do you think you can say yes to this question and yet doubt it all at the same time?

How have you seen God sustain or provide for other people in ways that have amazed you?

I think it's so easy to believe in God for others and struggle in believing in God for ourselves. We can see how God has provided for other people but when our deadline is fast approaching, we are pacing the halls like crazy. We can see how God serendipitously moved the chess pieces to make something happen so this person could meet that person to meet their "person," but when we are single and wanting not to be, it's hard to believe God will provide the desires of our heart. It's often hard to beleive for ourselves what we believe for others.

So often the **enemies** of our belief in a God who sustains us are just **stronger beliefs** in something else.

We believe God is too busy to *see* what's going on in our lives.

We believe God wants us to *learn* a lesson.

We believe God *cares* about people unlike us.

We believe God *thinks* we deserve this.

We believe God won't *answer* our prayers because we haven't done enough for Him.

We believe God isn't *capable*.

We believe God has *bigger* fish to fry.

Reflect

Go back to the statements on the previous page and circle the enemies of your belief that God can sustain you, provide for you, and take care of you.

What other beliefs do you often hold onto about God that keep you from believing He will meet you in your need?

Ruminate

As you battle the enemies of your belief in your personal Sustainer, meditate on these Scriptures:

I lie down and sleep; I wake again, because the Lord sustains me. **Psalm 3:5**

You make your saving help my shield, and your right hand sustains me; your help has made me great. **Psalm 18:35**

The Lord sustains them on their sickbed and restores them from their bed of illness. **Psalm 41:3**

Surely God is my help; the Lord is the one who sustains me. **Psalm 54:4**

He makes grass grow for the cattle, and plants for people to cultivate— bringing forth food from the earth: wine that gladdens human hearts, oil to make their faces shine, and bread that sustains their hearts. **Psalm 104:14-15**

The Lord watches over the foreigner and sustains the fatherless and the widow, but he frustrates the ways of the wicked. **Psalm 146:9**

The Lord sustains the humble but casts the wicked to the ground. **Psalm 147:6**

Put one of these verses in your pocket for the day. What I mean is, memorize it, hold onto it, write it down or keep it near in some way. As you go about your day, as soon as worry creeps in, pull the verse you chose out. Pull it out of your memory, your heart or your jean pocket and speak to what you worry about, these words, "No, you big stress ball, My God is a Sustainer."

Trusting in God to sustain us is an everyday battle. Worry and anxiety want to get you to a place of trusting no one. If they can isolate you to believe that you are the only one who can get you what you need, then you will be one big stresscase and guess who wins? Worry and anxiety win. We have to begin to be women who go outside, who look around, who remind ourselves of what is true. And what is true is that we have a God who promises to sustain who and what He has made. So in our cubicles and our carpools, let us look at the birds. In our need and in our want, let us look at the birds. In our desperation and our darkness, let us look at the birds. In our kitchens and in the corporate world, let us look at the birds. In our old age, our middle age and our college age years, let us look at the birds.

Worry finds us, so we must, in its midst, go finding God. We must look for God, claim God, trust God, talk to God, point to God, reflect on God, praise God, count on God, meditate on God, and find our peace in God. Worry has a way of convincing us that all of our worst fears will become a reality. Worry will find you. Go finding God. That's what Jesus is suggesting- shift what you look at. Don't just let your fear boss you around. Don't let stress overcome you. Don't let your anxiety get you pacing down some hypothetical bunny trail that might not end up being your reality. No, you go looking for what is real - your God. You go find Him. God is nearer to you than the worry that stops by to visit. Don't give your worry more power than you give your God. As soon as you start to get anxious, making up stories, pacing, biting your nails, drinking to self soothe, gossiping to take out an enemy, overworking to keep your worry from becoming a reality, or writing the next chapter before it's even begun, go finding God.

When you go finding something, you look for it with intensity. When you go finding something, you think about where you last saw it, and you return there. When you go finding something, you call its name. When you go finding something, you turn over everything it might be under. Find God with the same ferocity that worry finds you and I promise you, One shall overcome the other. And when it does, His peace shall surpass your understanding, His presence shall kick out your fear, and His promises shall be your hope.

When worry finds you, you go finding God.

Respond

Here is a fun homework assignment for you! It is so hard as women to find time and space to just "be." We rarely have time to spend wandering, hiking, or look for shooting stars. Challenge yourself in the next week to spend time outside looking for God- even if for 5 minutes, 5 hours or 5 days. I give you permission. Blame me. Go walk by the ocean and pay attention to the sound of the waves. Who tells the tide to come in and go out? Build a campfire and sit under the stars. They are the work of Whose fingers? Sit on a park bench and look at that bird. The same God who feeds the bluebird promises to be all that we need. Sit in His sufficiency and His sustenance. Make time and go looking for the sparrows. It is there you will find your God.

SIT IN HIS *sufficiency* AND HIS *sustenance.*

Your Story

Shelley

We encourage women to bravely and authentically tell their stories as they really are. We hope this "your story" meets you in yours.

Eighteen months ago, I was sitting in a meeting about our foster daughter, who was 20 months old at the time. I was there just to listen in, to perhaps see the progress of her mother, who was very pregnant at the time, and hear where the case was headed. During the course of the meeting I learned that the unborn baby would be removed from her mother's care when it was born. There had been no progress. I was shocked. I was not expecting this news at all. Neither was she. There were tears. Confusion. Anger. And by the end of the two-hour meeting (during which I was unable to reach my husband!), I had agreed to be the temporary placement home for the newborn.

I was 50 years old at this point, with four children ranging from the age of 15 years old to 22 years old, plus our 20-month old foster daughter who we had cared for during the previous six months. I was trying to wrap my head around it all. We were leaving that night for a conference and wouldn't be back for six days. I told my husband on the way to the airport (straight after the meeting) that I had agreed to take in the baby for two weeks to two months. He told me to call and cancel my agreement. The offices were closed. I texted my small group to pray for this entire crazy situation. What had I said YES to this time? I didn't want her to go into the system when her biological sister was with us. It was a pretty rough time.

So, we talked and prayed together for the next few days. I told my husband I was ready to do everything the baby needed and felt like God had confirmed my YES. I also told him I would do everything until God confirmed it in his heart as well. It was a whole lot of crazy and faith and trust and leaping into the unknown. We didn't have baby things. We didn't have a shower, or several, to welcome this sweet baby. We didn't have a room ready. We didn't have a car seat or outfit to come home in! What was I thinking? I was thinking that this man I was married to for

25 years thought I was crazy. And that he just may be right! But, I said I would keep my word and love the baby super well, like she was my own, for two weeks to two months. I would say YES and pray, pray, pray for PROVISION.

When we arrived home, I walked into my living room to find a bassinet, cubicles filled with baby clothes, homemade blankets, hats, diapers, wipes, formula, a swing, bibs, bottles… I cried. A lot. While standing there crying about the love of my small group who didn't just pray for my new crazy (they DID something and they all said YES with their resources by shopping and preparing for the baby while I was out of town), I received a call to go to the hospital. Baby girl was on the way! Biological mama wanted me there. Whirlwind. Emotions. Shock. Provision.

I went quickly and in a couple of hours I was holding a sweet 6lb 6oz baby girl. She didn't look a thing like my kids. She was tiny. She had so much hair. She didn't feel like mine. It didn't feel like I should even be there holding her. But I knew I was supposed to be there. I said YES to showing up, and yes to loving her well. I took her home two nights later. It felt surreal to drive her home, to stay up all night and hold her and rock her and cry with her. But God had provided all I needed and I didn't even come close to understanding how big of a deal that was yet. Everything is kind of a blur as I remember trying not to fall asleep as I prayed and prayed. What did all of this mean?

It meant, I said YES. It meant God was taking care of her needs through us. It also meant that He was taking care of our needs in ways I never dreamed. I bought NOTHING to bring her home. I bought no diapers for over a year. No formula for over a year. Diapers arrived on my doorstep and in the mail. New car seats in the mail. A crib dropped off. A rocking chair. More diapers. Toddler bed. Clothes and toys brought over or handed to us as we were out and about. More formula. Checks handed to us. I didn't ask for anything. I talked to Jesus about this sweet baby and prayed and prayed His will for her life. I was praying for her heart and mind, and He provided every physical need as well.

We still have both girls and we still pray for them daily. God has provided again and again. He has opened doors to the school district for me to love on more teen mamas because of having these girls. He has brought so many people into our world that we would have never known. Our heart for foster care has grown. We still are "temporary" unlicensed foster parents, but we are ALL in. God knows what is best for these girls and He has been holding them so beautifully in His hands. We said YES to Him using our hands to change diapers and feed bottles. We said YES to our arms rocking and swinging and bouncing cute girls. We said YES to our sleep being interrupted. We said YES to our older children learning to love and serve like none of us ever dreamed. We didn't even realize we were saying all of those YESES! God provided.

My husband is on board. He is passionate. He loves these girls deeply. He weeps over them. He rejoices with them. All of our kids are on board. We are all in. God continues to provide in crazy ways with daycare, clothes and other physical needs. I think we needed to see that physical, practical care in order to grasp the spiritual care He has for us. I don't worry about tomorrow. I don't worry about who the girls will be. I don't worry about any needs of food or clothing we have. I have open hands. They and ALL of their needs belong to Jesus right now. My heart has been ripped open like I never dreamed. God provides. He provides things. He provides love. He provides a way to talk to other people we never knew. He provides a home for sweet girls. He provides before we ask. I am so thankful that we have learned to see it in such a tangible way.

Written by Shelley Knebel

LOOK AT THE LILIES

Read

26 "Look at the birds of the air: they neither sow nor reap nor gather into barns, and yet your heavenly Father feeds them. Are you not of more value than they? 27 And which of you by being anxious can add a single hour to his span of life? 28 And why do you worry about clothing? Consider the lilies of the field, how they grow: they neither toil nor spin, 29 Yet I tell you, even Solomon in all his glory was not arrayed like one of these. 30 But if God so clothes the grass of the field, which today is alive and tomorrow is thrown into the oven, will he not much more clothe you, o you of little faith? 31 Therefore, do not be anxious, saying, 'What shall we eat?' or 'What shall we drink?' or 'What shall we wear?'" **Matthew 6:26-31(ESV)**

Jesus is a realist. He in a sense asks in verse 27, "What good does your worry do?" This question asks so many other questions. Are your sleepless nights working? Is your overtime making things better? Are the sleeping pills doing it for you? Are all your well laid plans making life perfect? Perhaps Jesus wants us to see how ineffective our worry is to change a single thing. He gets about as close as saying, "Worry isn't working for you."

Jesus suggests instead of worry, perhaps we should shift what we look at. Perspective is powerful when we view all of life's circumstances with an element of faith. We can gain insight from a portion of a story from Tauler, a German mystic. "One day Tauler met a beggar, 'God give you a good day, my friend,' he said. The beggar answered, 'I thank God I never had a bad one.' Then Tauler said, 'God give you a happy life, my friend.' 'I thank God,' said the beggar, 'I am never unhappy.' Tauler in amazement said, 'What do you mean?' 'Well,' said the beggar, 'when it is fine, I thank God; when it rains, I thank God; when I have plenty, I thank God; when I am hungry, I thank God; and since God's will is my will, and whatever pleases him pleases me, why should I say I am unhappy when I am not?' Tauler looked at the man in astonishment. 'Who are you?' he asked. 'I am a king,' said the beggar. 'Where then is your kingdom?' asked Tauler. And the beggar answered quietly: 'In my heart.' "[21]

Worry sees the beggar, faith sees the king. Worry sees the doom, faith sees the destiny. Worry sees the rain, faith sees the growing seed. Worry pushes God out of sight, faith pulls God back into view.

Barclay, W. (Ed.). (1976). *The Gospel of Matthew* (Vol. 1, pp. 260–261). Philadelphia, PA: The Westminster John Knox Press.

Reflect

What do you find interesting about Jesus trying to shift our perspective from looking at worry to looking at something else?

What practices do you do to shift your perspective in life from a place of worry to a place of faith?

What strikes you about the power of perspective in the story of the beggar?

If in the beggar's shoes, what would your outlook be?

Jesus not only says look at the birds but also look at the lilies. Gorgeous lilies would bloom randomly on the Palestinian hillsides and their beauty surpassed the wardrobe of the richest of royalty. And even still, when a woman needed to raise the heat in her clay oven to cook she would throw handfuls of dried grass and wildflowers inside so she could prepare a meal.[22] Jesus knew His audience would get that He was saying:

EVEN
THE
lilies
ARE
FOR
you.

It is like Jesus says, "If God cares so wonderfully for wildflowers that are here today and thrown into the fire tomorrow, will He not certainly care for you? Why do you have so little faith?" Do you see what Jesus is doing here in this passage? There seems to be a theme. In **Matthew 6:26-30**, Jesus poses a standard Jewish HOW MUCH MORE argument. [23]

God **values** the birds, how much more does He **value** you?
God **cares** for the lilies, how much more does He **care** for you?

JESUS IS DRAWING A CONNECTION BETWEEN
worry AND *value.*

22 Barclay, W. (Ed.). (1976). The Gospel of Matthew (Vol. 1, pp. 257–258). Philadelphia, PA: The Westminster John Knox Press.
23 Keener, C. S. (1993). The IVP Bible background commentary: New Testament (Mt 6:26–27). Downers Grove, IL: InterVarsity Press.

How insightful is our God! He knows that at the root of much of our anxiety and worry is this deep doubt that we might not be seen as valuable enough to be taken care of. Deep within us, if we could unlayer all the layers of worry, do we question that we will be seen, heard, provided for, worked for, prayed over, sustained, listened to, picked up, and walked alongside? Do we question this because we aren't sure we are valued and cared for enough by God and others?

I have heard a million sermons on worry, but never one that connected our anxiety to our sense of value. I am going to go with Jesus on this one. Jesus' sermon connects our worry directly to our sense of value. "How much more do I value you?" He asks. The deep root of most of our nail biting, fretting, pacing, stressing and hypothetical fears comes from a belief that we, in and of ourselves, are not valuable enough to be taken care of.

Reflect

Jesus passionately preached "look at the lilies." What do you think that said to women in this day and this culture?

What do you appreciate about Jesus not just saying "Do not worry," but instead connecting worry to our sense of value?

Write down the 3 biggest things you worry about today.

 1.

 2.

 3.

If you go back to those 3 things you are most worried about, how do you see a questioning of value playing into this worry?

 1.

 2.

 3.

Jesus asks 2 questions in this passage we should take the time to answer:

1. God values the birds, how much more does He value you?

2. God cares for the lilies, how much more does He care for you?

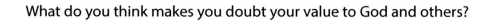

What do you think makes you doubt your value to God and others?

What kind of soul work do you think you can enter into to increase your God given sense of value?

This connection Jesus is drawing between worry and value seems so important that we want to sit in it for a while. We will spend the next few parts continuing the conversation.

Respond

Today, write a prayer in the space provided, asking the Lord to meet you in the places you have begun to question your value and ask God to replace and restore you with His truth, His love and His care for you.

God who feeds the birds and clothes the lilies,

Amen

Your Story

Kara

We encourage women to bravely and authentically tell their stories as they really are. We hope this "your story" meets you in yours.

If you were to have asked me even just a couple months ago about my anxiety, I would have had a very different response. I've been in and out of counseling since I was 14. Counselors, psychiatrists, the whole 9 years, trying to navigate clinical major depression and anxiety. For the most part I'd say I've had a handle on it, being used to living in a haze and bouts of self-harm episodes. If I could maintain an outgoing persona then it really can't be that bad, right? It wasn't until I had a really severe 'low' that I realized I can't continue to be complacent toward my mental health. It sounds obvious, but it's pretty hard to pretend like you're not drowning when you actually are.

Recently, I began seeing a new counselor who taught me how to put words to the static I feel in my brain, and I hope you find these words encouraging as well.

○ God did not give me depression to punish me. Yes I do have a chemical imbalance in my brain, but it's not because I did anything wrong.

○ Some days I can handle more than on other days, and there is no shame in having a different capacity than someone else. There are still days that I just have to push through to push through, but I am also allowed to establish boundaries so I can be present when I need to be

○ I cry a lot and that's just how it is. #teamtears

○ Having depression and loving Jesus are not mutually exclusive. Living out your faith is not ignoring your mental health. Jesus weeps when you weep, He hurts when you hurt, and He sits in your depression and anxiety with you. Depression is not the absence of the Lord, but an opportunity to experience His compassion

○ I am in process always and that is OKAY. We do not need to wait until we have it all figured out to start telling our story. You are whole because Jesus made you whole and where you're at in your story doesn't change that.

○ We are continually going to places we've never been before, and you are allowed to not get it right the first time.

○ "I am not enough" does not have to be your path of least resistance. Walk in your enoughness until the path of unworthiness grows over. This is a long process and it's going to be easier to go back to the 'not enough' path if you've been walking in it for awhile.

○ "Do not worry" does not mean ignore the worry. However, we can learn to hold it differently. Jesus holds you while you hold your worry. Whatever fears, doubts, concerns, hypothetical scenarios, real scenarios, anxieties that you have, know that God is bigger.

○ Mental illness looks different for everyone, and what you feel is REAL.

○ You can live with your anxiety and not in spite of it. As long as anxiety and depression exists, Jesus is going to use it for the kingdom. There will still be days that feel like you're trying to run through water, but since you've walked through it, you walk with other people through it too.

I am still in process, I am still in the middle of my story, and there are still days where I don't fully trust the Lord. But I know that my distrust doesn't scare Him away. And as long as I keep running toward Jesus, no matter how slow, He is running toward me too. I am precious and His beloved in the midst of all the messiness. And so are you.

Written by Kara Eckardt

STOLEN VALUE

It is an interesting idea that our sense of value is perhaps connected to a lot of worry's root and worry's cure. If we don't have any other conversation regarding worry, we have to have this one: Have you forgotten your value? Who stole it from you? Our value can be pickpocketed without us even noticing. It can be abducted twenty years prior to realizing it's gone. Value can be ransacked in one experience and it can be embezzled over the course of time. It can be snitched by our closest friends, our biggest enemies and the enemy. Value can be pilfered by words, circumstances, trauma, and absence. Value can be taken when we're 100 and when we're 10.

We are going to spend some time walking through 6 ways our sense of value can be taken from us. (I am sure there are a million, but we will start with these.) As we walk through these, consider how they resonate with you, and if not you, those around you.

1 Our sense of value is stolen the day fear breaks in and says, "You should be afraid."

10, that's how old I was when I laid in my bed home alone hoping to fall asleep. I heard a noise. Someone was breaking in through the bathroom window. I stiffened. It was him. The man who took his rage out on us. He was back. He found his way into our new place. I laid still, hoping he wouldn't realize I lay there. Without moving, my mind raced. What could I do? There was no cell phone to call for help. There was no strength that could match his. There was no parent to step in and defend. This, friends, is when fear moved into me and it's step brother Worry got a room too.

Reflect

Can you think of a moment or moments, when fear broke into your life and told you that you should be afraid?

How do you experience an old legitimate fear now creating new reasons to fear (that may or may not be legitimate)?

How do you think those fearful experiences stole your sense of value?

Who or what stole your value when they told you to be afraid?

Part of walking toward healing in our lives is naming things. We need to name who or what stole our value. I know it's hard. I know that if we see their name written down or we go there and recall the memory, it all floods back. It feels like we are experiencing it all over again. But we have to name it. We like to say around Collide, "You have to recognize brokenness before it can be made whole." If we want to move past the anxiety that has been birthed by fear, then we have to start by naming it and claiming it. It is then we can invite Jesus into it. We can't invite Jesus to heal wounds we pretend aren't bleeding. We can't invite Jesus to help us forgive someone we refuse to name. We can't invite Jesus to give us courage when we fail to name our fears. As we've already chatted about, **God wants to replace our fear with freedom** and sometimes it starts by naming it.

So I will ask it again, in case you need more prodding, who or what stole your value when they told you with their words, their actions or their inaction, "You should be afraid"?

Our sense of value can get lost in a circumstance in life that leaves a void.

11 was how old my friend was when her mom had cancer. She went in for surgery and didn't come out. Blank pages in a story that should write words, sentences, paragraphs and chapters telling of experience, adventure, and memories. No mom when my friend started her period or needed boy advice. No mom at prom or the mother daughter tea. No mom at graduation or her wedding. No prayers at bedtime. No mom's favorite recipe. No "I love you to the moon and back."

God doesn't want to leave us in the emptiness and void that absence and death and divorce have left. Some of you have been wondering the answers to your questions for far too long. Was I loved? Do they long for me like I long for them? Do they think of me? Why didn't they show up? Do I look like them? Would we be close? God knows our story, He hears our cries and **God wants to restore everything we have lost.**

Hold onto this promise: **Deuteronomy 30:3** in the The Message Bible says, *"God, your God, will restore everything you lost; he'll have compassion on you; he'll come back and pick up the pieces from all the places where you were scattered."*

Reflect

What do you desire to be restored?

What have you lost?

What has been scattered?

What does God promise to do according to **Deuteronomy 30:3**?

3 Our sense of value is stripped when we begin to believe, "People won't choose me."

12 year old sweet Madeline walked up to a circle of girls and one said, "Who do you guys like better, Jenny or Madeline?" One by one, each girl said,

"Jenny."

"Jenny."

"Jenny."

Not one girl who was supposed to be Madeline's friend said, "I like them both." or, "I'm not playing this stupid game." It's so easy to walk away from these kinds of circles into new ones questioning our worth.

God doesn't want any girl in any circle to walk away feeling as though they are not worthy of being chosen or stood up for. **God wants for all of us, belonging.** If you've been a victim of bullying, if you've been sideswiped by mean girls or mean women (because somehow this happens all the time in adult circles too), if you've been isolated, if you've been made to feel as though you're not good enough for the cool kids club, God wants to set you straight. The cool kids are standing in circles where everyone belongs and any circle you're not cool enough to stand in is a circle Jesus was already pushed out of.

Reflect

How does Madeline's story resonate with yours?

97

Describe the experiences you have had either feeling pushed out of what I call a "cool kids club" or being the one pushing people out to try and look "cool".

How do you think your experience impacts the way you now carry out relationships?

Our sense of value is robbed when we inflict a grudge upon ourselves for things we cannot forgive, that God does forgive.

30, and someone I sat across from at a coffee shop was mourning the loss of her baby that didn't make it to full term. She groaned in grief. She was having anxiety attacks. She hadn't gone back to work and she couldn't stop crying. I stood there listening as more than grief started coming out. She had terminated several pregnancies years before. She said this loss was her fault. Because of her past regrets she was now blaming herself. It was easier for her to hate herself than it was to lean into grace. Her faith in God's care for her was stripped the day she decided she couldn't forgive herself.

And you know what? God doesn't want us drowning ourselves in our own unforgiveness. Enough of beating yourself over the head anymore, ladies. God wants to set you free from the ways you are holding yourself captive. **God wants for us grace.**

Reflect

What have you not been able to forgive yourself for?

Have you asked God for forgiveness? If so, why can you not let go of the very thing God has?

I'd like to take a moment to explain the simplicity of God's heart. **1 John 1:9** says, *"If we confess our sins, he is faithful and just and will forgive us our sins and purify us from all unrighteousness."* Confession looks just like this:

"God I confess that I blew it when I (fill in the blank with whatever monstrosity of a sin you committed that you can't seem to let go of). And God I need you to forgive me."

Boom. Forgiven. You know, a lot of us have spent decades of our lives trying to make up for one night stands, abortions, addictions, lies, selfishness and greed. And in a meta moment God will relinquish all of it. All we have to do is come before the One who holds the greatest storehouse of grace we could ever imagine. And He showers our self inflicted unforgiveness with a grace that washes us free and clean. **Isaiah 1:18** tells us that God will turn what is scarlet white as snow.

There is no more blood. No more torture. No more suffering. Jesus took all that on - on the cross. So stop taking away the life-giving, redemptive, forever freeing work Jesus did for you.

STOP TAKING AWAY THE LIFE-GIVING, REDEMPTIVE, forever freeing work JESUS DID FOR YOU.

99

Once you confess, just say, "Thank you." Let's all stop being so hard on ourselves and let's all stop over-complicating what Jesus made simple through what was, for Him, so very, very difficult. **Isaiah 53:5** assures us that our God,

"HE WAS PIERCED FOR OUR TRANSGRESSIONS,
HE WAS CRUSHED FOR OUR INIQUITIES;
THE PUNISHMENT THAT BROUGHT US PEACE WAS ON HIM,
AND *by His wounds we are healed*"

Live into God's forgiveness as though you believe it be real. And real will be your peace, your freedom and your joy that have all been covered up and smothered by the life sucking, joy killing, spirit crushing enemy that is self unforgiveness. It's been way too long, friend.

5   Our sense of value is taken when people whose value has been stolen, try stealing ours.

50, and wondering why he was gone all the time. She tracked his phone bill. She followed his every move on her iPhone. She became obsessed. Her worst fear became her reality. He was with someone else. Fifteen years of marriage. He said he was no longer in love. "She's more like a friend." She wasn't enough to stay. She tried to be. The empty closet, the cold side of the right side of the bed, the missing seat at the dinner table. She still wears his last name. She wishes he wanted her to.

100

Some of you have been robbed. Someone who felt weak tried to overpower you. Someone who was insecure tried to steal your security. Someone who was scared tried to frighten you so they wouldn't be alone. Someone who wanted family tried to take yours. And you know what? Jesus loves thieves, He died next to <u>two</u>, made friends with <u>one</u>, but wants <u>zero</u> to take from you because someone took from them. **God wants a thief to come to Him to get their value back instead of robbing yours.**

Reflect

How can you begin to see that when people steal your value it is because someone has stolen theirs?

When you view people this way, what does that change for you as you relate to those who have hurt you?

JESUS LOVES *Thieves*, HE DIED NEXT TO TWO, MADE FRIENDS WITH ONE, BUT WANTS ZERO TO TAKE FROM YOU BECAUSE SOMEONE TOOK FROM THEM.

Has someone stolen your value because someone stole theirs? If so, who stole theirs?

How do you feel about the idea that God wants to give all people back their value, including you and the person who hurt you?

Our sense of value is plundered the minute we buy into broken theology that questions God's care for us.

70, and her religious community told her that her son who had just committed suicide was in hell. The message she heard was, "God thinks despair and mental illness deserve torture." That was the day she left the church with no plans to come back.

Another woman I know married into Christian in-laws who told her, ever so sweetly, they didn't intend to spend holidays with her relatives because of their "past." The message conveyed was, "God doesn't do sinners."

A friend of mine lost her mom in a tragic accident as a teenager and a church leader forced her to sit in a room by herself after her mother's funeral to "think about things." The message this grieving daughter heard was, "God wants you to feel guilty."

You know what this is? Broken theology. I've seen it countless times. **Broken theology** lies to us about God. And every lie makes us question our value and God's. And God sure as heck doesn't want us believing broken ideas about Him that in turn make us believe broken things about ourselves.

It's broken theology to communicate, "God thinks despair and mental illness deserve torture." That's not the God I know. The God I know walks into tombs to collide with people who are isolated by cutting, depression and demon possession.

It's broken theology to act as though "God doesn't do sinners." Jesus said I came for who? "Snobby, uptight, perfect, straight A, rule following, healthy, put together, Bible trivia winners"? No, He said, "I came for sinners. Let's have dinners."

It's broken theology to suggest, "God wants you to feel guilty." I'm pretty sure God wants you to feel guilt free. If God wanted my friend as a child in a room for hours after her mother's funeral, it would have been to hold her and tell her He loved her. But instead she sat there damned in grief. She's 40 now and the last place you'll find her is in a church. **God wants us to know Him authentically, as He really is, not as others make Him out to be.** The Bible says if you wanna know what God is like, look at Jesus.

Reflect

If broken theology lies to us about who we are and who God is, how have you been lied to?

JESUS *wants* TO GIVE YOU YOUR *value* BACK.

Jesus suggests we look at Him if we want to know what God is like. Describe what God seems like when you look at Jesus.

Jesus wants us to know Him as He really is, not as we want Him to be and not as others make Him out to be. How can you best know Jesus for who He says He is?

When Jesus ran into people in the New Testament He gave people back their value. Jesus went out of His way to meet the woman at the well who was seen as a get-around-girl and He reminded her that her life was so valuable that she deserved more than she was giving her life credit for. When Jesus showed up at the synagogue and healed a woman who was bent over in spirit, the religious schmucks complained that He had done this on the Sabbath. Jesus not only defended her worthiness of such an act but He also called her "Daughter." Jesus looked these guys straight square in the eyes and called them out. It was like He said, "You would even pull an ass (the King James version uses this word, so I can too.) out of a ditch on the Sabbath, but is this woman not worth so much more?" Jesus shows up on people's scenes all the time to give them back their value. And He wants to do that with you and with me.

Ruminate

Look up the following collisions where Jesus collides with someone who has lost their sense of value. In the table below, describe who or what stole their value and how Jesus gave it back.

Scripture	Person who lost their sense of value	Who or what stole their value?	How did Jesus give back their value?
Mark 5:1-20	demon-possessed man in tombs cutting himself	mental illness, community isolation and people's judgment, self inflicted torture	Jesus went out of his way to meet him. Community isolated him but Jesus pursued him.
Luke 7:36-50	"sinful woman"		Jesus honored her in a room full of haters.
Luke 13:10-17			
John 4:4-26	Samaritan woman at the well		
John 5:1-14			

What stands out to you about Jesus and His interactions with people who lost their sense of value?

How do you see Jesus giving people back their sense of value?

SOMEONE STOLE MY *value*
AND I WANT IT BACK!
AND SOMEONE STOLE YOURS
AND GOD WANTS TO RETURN IT!

Let me tell you about the God I know. God wants to replace your fear with courage. God wants to replace your worry with peace. God doesn't want you anxious about what will happen next. I don't care who or what put fear into you, God is bigger, God is stronger, and God is to be feared. And my God, He values you too much to let some fear-bringer take down your life. God doesn't want you to keep thinking you need to worry and be afraid all the time any more than He wants me to still be that 10 year old girl. There is a good chance this section has brought up some pain and woundedness that still need healing, and so might the next section. If you are sensing the need to process with a counselor, please see page 120 to get more information about seeking counseling.

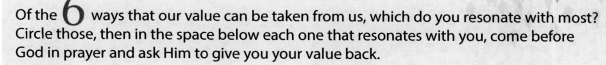

Respond

Of the **6** ways that our value can be taken from us, which do you resonate with most? Circle those, then in the space below each one that resonates with you, come before God in prayer and ask Him to give you your value back.

1 Our sense of value is stolen the day fear breaks in and says, "You should be afraid."

God . . .

2 Our sense of value can get lost in a circumstance in life that leaves a void.

God . . .

3 Our sense of value is stripped when we begin to believe, "People won't choose me."

God . . .

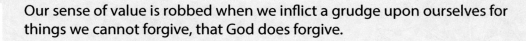

4 Our sense of value is robbed when we inflict a grudge upon ourselves for things we cannot forgive, that God does forgive.

God . . .

5 Our sense of value is taken when people whose value has been stolen, try stealing ours.

God . . .

6 Our sense of value is plundered the minute we buy into broken theology that questions God's care for us.

God . . .

Counselor's Couch
Breeze Potts

Our sense of value, how much we feel we can add meaning and purpose to the world and the lives around us, can be distorted when we are worried and/or anxious. When the subject of one's value comes up in my office (and it does regularly), it is imperative that the client and I together consider value distortions and evaluate whether or not they are accurate. It is my experience, both personally and professionally, that distortions feel like truth, but they are far from it. I started doing this work because I was a client first. I was the one in the counselor's office sorting through my own cognitive distortions. It is a great honor to now be able to help people, through my counseling practice, to live out the most authentic versions of themselves that they can. I believe this continues to develop over time as we continue to grow, change and be transformed by our own awareness, but also by the relationships we are in and the love of God leading us to be more like Himself.

Cognitive distortions cause us to lose our way emotionally, spiritually and physically. Distortions sound familiar; they often communicate some of what we fear most: we aren't worth it (it being defined as another person's energy, time or effort). Distortions can fill our mind with worry about the "what ifs" of the future and fill our hearts with doubt and regret about the past. They seek to inform who we are, but distortions are like looking at ourselves in a carnival mirror. The mirrored image bears resemblance but is a misrepresented version of who we are. The problem arises when we begin to believe that the distorted image is an accurate reflection and we begin to see ourselves through the lens of something that was never meant to be truth. Distortions lie, deceive and steal joy. Wounds that aren't tended to have a habit of festering and causing systemic infection. The byproduct of this emotionally systemic infection is that we come to believe altered facts about who we are based on what our wound tells us. These are distortions.

When a client and I uncover a possible cognitive distortion in session, I begin by asking the client to consider what value messages they are receiving by entertaining those thoughts. We look at this honestly and consider the emotional impact it's having on their identity. I also challenge the validity of the message by considering where it is coming from. What is it connected to? Is the source reliable? Does it speak truth? We consider if there are other ways of hearing the message. Are there other perspectives or possible explanations of intent? As a therapist, I want to consider whether or not the value messages can be directly clarified. Is there a possible misunderstanding? Would it be possible to go back to the relationship and seek clarity? If this is possible, is the client able and willing? We can be able and we can be willing, but I think it's important to consider where we are both able and willing at the same moment. It is also important to consider the risk; what is required of us? But also, perhaps more importantly, it is important to consider what might be gained.

I have also found it helpful to encourage a client to consider what they might think, feel and/or say if one of their friends was expressing the same distortion that the client is expressing to me. This is not a favorite tool among my clients, but a helpful one because it helps access a level of self-compassion that the distortion itself prevents us from accessing. Self-compassion is the antidote to the festering wounds and the cognitive lies we've believed. It is the tool that helps our hearts soften toward ourselves so we can begin to access the truth of who God says we are.

In addition to the processing and dialogue that I hope bring some relief from the cognitive trap, I often find myself recommending a few very practical strategies that can be used to decrease stress and anxiety and help a client feel calmer. This helps the therapy process by allowing a client to feel more hopeful that change is possible and more empowered to make those changes. The following strategies are things I have collected over time but have continued to recommend over and over again because they are the tools clients repeatedly tell me are helpful. As I recommend them in my office, many clients seem skeptical. These are often the same clients who communicate surprise when they do try them and find they actually help. I always tell my clients that I don't have anything magic or any band aid solutions, but that these tools are a way of working with ourselves to alleviate our distress and something we can come back to later in life if other challenging or distressing circumstances present themselves.

1. Free write exercise:
Set a timer for 5-10 minutes and write out any thought that comes to mind during the time period. Write thoughts, emotions, to do lists, etc. Write with pen and paper, write quickly, write ugly, do not worry about spelling or grammar, do not edit. Focus on getting thoughts out and away from you. When the timer goes off, finish writing any remaining thoughts and destroy the paper. Once the paper is destroyed, get up and do something else (take a shower, go for a walk, call a friend, get a snack, pet your dog, etc.). Do not sit where you are and think about all the things you wrote. Physically moving locations will help your body and mind let go of what you just processed.

2. Breathing exercises:
 4-4-8   Inhale through your nose, exhale through your mouth. Inhale for the count of 4, hold for the count of 4, exhale for the count of 8. Do this until you feel calmer. Imagine that you are blowing your stress away from you when you exhale.

Box Breathing   Trace a box with your index finger somewhere (paper, table, arm or leg, steering wheel, etc.). As you go up the left side, inhale through your nose, and you go across the top of the square, hold, as you come down the right side, exhale through your mouth and as you draw the bottom line to form the square just rest and reflect on how you're doing. This exercise does not have a set cadence but I encourage a slow steady rhythm. Do this until you feel calmer.

3. Take a 20-minute walk (stroll) and focus on what you see.

4. Write down 5 things you're thankful for each day and tell someone about them.

5. Write down 3-5 things that are positive about you (internal and external characteristics) and say them out loud to yourself daily.

6. Work on sleep hygiene, find a regular sleep rhythm (earlier to bed, earlier to rise is ideal, but be gentle with yourself. Make small changes and focus on getting quality sleep).

7. Engage in aerobic exercise (45 min or longer) 3-5 times per week.

All of these tools and strategies are forms of self care that help us prioritize our own value. They don't always immediately make us feel more valued, but with practice they will give us a sense of groundedness and build a strong foundation upon which our value can be more fully realized. I find that often times, it is the seemingly "simple" things that have such a profound impact. Breathing, eating, sleeping...these are all things we do "naturally" and yet when we are distressed, they are some of the first things disrupted so it is important that we are intentional about doing the simple tasks well. My exercise instructors often say, "you have to give energy to gain energy." This is very true in my workout experience. I can go through the motions and not give much, but when I leave, I haven't gained much either. But when I give my effort in my workout, I walk out of class feeling energized, rejuvenated. I would like to suggest that I believe the same philosophy is true in mental and emotional health. We have to put forth some effort to bring about change, or no change happens. Change is only change when something changes. And the way we can begin to change how we view ourselves, is by taking care of ourselves, and making space for us to see ourselves differently than we have before.

Written by Breeze Potts, MA

BACKWARD TO GO FORWARD

8

Jesus wants to replace the value that has been taken from you. He seems certain that if you are sure of your value, you will be far less anxious. But here is the deal:

SOMETIMES YOU HAVE TO GO

BACKWARD TO GO *forward.*

You don't want to hear that do you? I'm telling you what, you can't move forward and act as though it didn't happen.

That's called a cover up, not a healing.

You aren't immortal. Sticks and stones break your bones and names do hurt you. You're not immune. You can't just move on when someone takes what is intrinsically yours. You're too valuable not to be protected, cared for and respected. Your past runs faster than you do. You need to allow the God who cares about you to go backward with you to the places and spaces where your value was stolen.

You have to let the God who collides, meet you there.

Some of you need to go backward to go forward. Maybe you only need to go as far back as last week, and maybe it's not traumatic, maybe it feels small. But if it's profound enough to travel forward, then it's gonna be profound enough to need to return back. Some of you, need to go way back and you need to invite God to go there too. God wants to stitch you up in the places that need stitching. God wants to stop your hemorrhaging. God wants to give you new names. But you have to allow Him to meet you. He can't heal you if you're hiding your wounds. He can't do surgery if you are gonna act as though you don't need it. He can't replace your value unless you recognize it was stolen. Going backward to go forward can happen in a counseling office. It can happen in prayer. It can happen in a trusted friendship or a great church community. And it can happen here in this study.

IF IT'S *profound enough* TO TRAVEL FORWARD, THEN IT'S GONNA BE PROFOUND ENOUGH TO NEED TO RETURN BACK.

I recently sat with a teenage girl I am pulling for in a big way. I know what's going on in her life and when I asked her how she was doing, she said, "I'm fine," with an "I'm trying to convince you" smile. I called her on it, "There's too much on the line," I said. "You have too great a future ahead of you. God's got a destiny and a calling for your life. And I'm worried that you're gonna move on from this circumstance just trying to survive and it's gonna follow you and mess with the amazing life God has for you." Her "I'm fine" melted into tears. I pleaded with her, "If you experience pain, trauma, secrets, or family dysfunction and you don't deal with it, it's going to walk you right into your twenties, your thirties and so on. You can sweep it under a rug, but you know what happens? It layers and layers and the next thing you know - it doesn't look like a rug anymore."

Reflect

How often do you try to put your chin up and move on from something painful without evaluating its effects?

Circle which of the following you find yourself doing when facing hard things:

- ◯ I sweep things under the rug.

- ◯ I pretend they aren't happening.

- ◯ I deflect the situation and talk to people about what's going on with them so I don't have to hide what's going on with me.

- ◯ I make up lies so I don't have to share the truth.

- ◯ I stay busy so I don't have to face reality.

- ◯ I say, "I'm fine," even when that's the farthest thing from true.

- ◯ I choose to live in someone else's pretend world of denial.

- ◯ I enable the circumstance because I don't know what else to do.

- ◯ I stay "cozy" in the dysfunction because I don't know who I'd be without it.

- ◯ Other: _____

When people sweep things under a rug, what have you seen end up happening?

Are there things you have swept under a rug that you are sensing you need to deal with?

Who are you trying to protect by not dealing with it?

Ruminate

Read the following verses and let them soak in as you consider the ways you or others around you have swept things under rugs. Listen for what the Lord might be telling you.

Nothing is covered up that will not be revealed, or hidden that will not be known. **Luke 12:2 (ESV)**

For nothing is hidden that will not be made manifest, nor is anything secret that will not be known and come to light. **Luke 8:17 (ESV)**

> ^{26}So have no fear of them, for nothing is covered that will not be revealed, or hidden that will not be known. ^{27}What I tell you in the dark, say in the light, and what you hear whispered, proclaim on the housetops. ^{28}And do not fear those who kill the body but cannot kill the soul. Rather fear him who can destroy both soul and body in hell.
> **Matthew 10:26-28 (ESV)**

When I was twenty-one years old and had just met Jesus, I sat in an office with a Christian counselor who could see there was a lot of healing that needed to take place in my life. One session she asked me to go back to a sad place as a child. You know what…I could have told her some real doozies, but guess what I saw? I very simply saw myself sitting on an old tattered, plum colored, velvet chair in our house by myself. I was alone, wanting not to be. The loneliness was saying, "You deserve to be alone. You will always be left for something better."

The day I was able to bravely go backward and start processing my story, telling my secrets, assessing my pain, and owning my mess-ups was the beginning of me moving forward. I had to invite Jesus to sit with me on that chair, and when I did, He began to restore my sense of value.

Reflect

Can you think back to a time where you keenly sense that your value was taken from you? If so what happened?

Take a moment and return back to the scene and take in the colors, the smells, the sights and the sounds. How did you feel then?

How do you feel now, just thinking about it?

Can you recognize what you needed in that moment? Take time to describe…

Can you be brave and ask God to meet you back there and give you now what you needed then?

Jesus wants to return to the hard spots with you. The invitation and request of His presence in and of itself begins to bring healing. Inviting God to return to old wounds is one of the bravest things I think a woman can ever do.

Keep being brave, friend.

I walked out of my office the other day and ran into a lady in the hall who asked what Collide was and the next thing I knew, she was crying on a chair across from me. She shared about her marriage in crisis. Her husband no longer sleeps in their bedroom or pays attention to her. I could see that her sense of value had been stripped by his lack of interest and engagement. She said, "I've been a Christian for years but I don't know how to invite God into this mess." I looked at her and said, "You're doing it." I grabbed her hands and I invited God to come into her family's mess, knowing He is a God who is in the house cleaning business. Going backward to go forward always looks like inviting God into the pain, the trauma, the mistakes, the moment a thief came in and stole from you.

117

GOING BACKWARD TO GO FORWARD ALWAYS LOOKS LIKE INVITING GOD INTO THE PAIN, THE TRAUMA, THE MISTAKES, THE *moment* A THIEF CAME IN AND STOLE FROM YOU.

Reflect

Can you resonate with not knowing how to invite God into your mess?

What do you think it looks like to invite a friend or family member into what is going on in your life?

What are some practical ways you can invite God into the "rooms of your house" that need some upkeep, cleaning and help?

So many of us have been plagued by worry. Jesus seems to draw a pretty clear line from our worry to our sense of value. One of the most courageous moves we can make is to return to the scene of the crime when our sense of value was taken from us. We need to stare that criminal right in the eyes! We need God to go back there with us and bring healing, insight, hope and new words of life to replace the old words that brought death. Jesus wants to move us forward but we need to join Him on the road toward healing. No more sweeping things under the rug hoping they go away! No more pretending it didn't happen! No more acting as though we don't need what we desperately do! No more locking God out of the doors of our house! A value full, worry free life is found when we invite our God to enter the pain and walk alongside us toward the hope.

Respond

Pray along with me…

God,

My ever-present help in trouble, help me be present to my own troubles. Help me to not sweep things under the rug but to live wide open to what Your light can handle. Jesus come into my mess and my pain. I hear You are pretty great at cleaning things up and I need a little help around here. I need You to restore everything that has been taken from me. Give me my value back, Lord. It has been taken from me and I want it back. I want to be certain in my inmost being that I am valued, so I no longer need to worry that I will be taken care of. Give me the courage I need to return to old wounds, visit present insecurities, and speak to elephants in the room so that I can be restored. I will trust that You will walk with me and be all that I need.

Amen

Seeking Counseling

We have been processing some hard stuff up until this point. If along the way you are feeling like there is more to process, seeking out someone to dialogue with about it could be a brave and good thing to do! I strongly suggest considering a counselor. Counseling has been something that God has used in my life to further walk me down the road toward healing and I think it could be the same for you. So often we need to make space and time for God to heal the places that have been deeply wounded. We wanted to lay out for you some common questions we get around counseling and hopefully the answers will be helpful as you seek out God's help and healing in your life.

How do I know if I need to see a counselor?

Making the choice to work with a counselor is a personal choice, and can be made for a variety of reasons. You may want to work with a counselor if you are facing some form of crisis, dealing with a loss in your life or experiencing strain in a relationship with a friend or family member. You may also want to seek counseling because you are interested in better understanding yourself and the way you relate to others. Choosing to work with a counselor is an act of self discovery and a step towards transformation. Working with a counselor can help bring clarity to places of confusion, provide tools to help you be more holistically and spiritually healthy, and help provide a place to grow in understanding of yourself and who you aspire to be.

What questions do I ask to find a counselor who is right for me?

A "good fit" between the therapist and the client is an essential part of the therapy process. A good connection between counselor and client provides the rich framework upon all that will happen during the counseling process. Therefore, it is important that a client is able to meet briefly with a counselor, or talk to them on the phone to get a "gut sense" of whether or not this counselor will be able to help the client achieve their counseling goals. While there is not a list of questions that will suit everyone's needs, we have compiled a list that may be beneficial to ask a counselor:

- What is the counselor's area of specialty?

- What experience/training do they have that has helped them in their area of specialty?

- What treatment modalities does the counselor draw upon? Ask them to share about treatment options.

- How will the counselor help determine when a client is done?

- What is expected of the client during the counseling process?

- What can the client expect to receive from counseling?

For more information go to wecollide.net/counseling

GOD TAKES MATTERS INTO HIS OWN HANDS

We have a God who puts His money where His mouth is. Jesus doesn't just say He values us, He takes matters into His own hands to prove it. In more than 200 places the Bible speaks of God's hand, which is always about God's activity in which He shows Himself to be alive and well.[24]

Ruminate

Read the following and circle what God has accomplished with His hand:

GOD CREATES WITH HIS HANDS:

God established the Earth with His hand. **Isaiah 45:12**

The Heavens are the work of His hands. **Psalm 102:25**

The rich and the poor, all, are the works of His hands. **Job 34:19**

GOD RESCUES WITH HIS HANDS:

God took the Israelites by the hand. **Hebrews 8:9**

God has bared His holy arm to show His salvation. **Isaiah 52:10**

By a powerful hand the Lord brought the Israelites out of slavery. **Exodus 13:3**

The Lord saves the Israelites with a mighty hand and anoutstretched arm. **Deuteronomy 5:15**

GOD'S HAND LACKS NOTHING:

Surely the arm of the LORD is not too short to save, nor his ear too dull to hear. **Isaiah 59:1**

Your hand is strong, your right hand is exalted. **Psalm 89:13**

The works of his hands are faithful and just; all his precepts are trustworthy. **Psalm 111:7**

GOD'S HAND EMPOWERS PEOPLE:

His hand empowers Elijah. **1 Kings 18:46**

His hand commandeers Ezekiel. **Ezekiel 1:3**

24 G. Kittel, G. W. Bromiley, & G. Friedrich (Eds.), Theological dictionary of the New Testament (electronic ed., Vol. 9, p. 427). Grand Rapids, MI: Eerdmans.

GOD'S HAND HEALS PEOPLE:

Jesus touched the sick and they were cured. **Luke 4:40**

Jesus laid hands on a deaf mute and healed him. **Mark 7:32-35**

Jesus spit on the ground, made mud and with his fingers put it on a blind man's eyes and restored his sight. **John 9:6**

Jesus healed the epileptic boy and handed him back to his father. **Luke 9:42-43**

Jesus touched a woman who was bent over by a spirit getting her down for decades and she was set free and standing straight in dignity. **Luke 13:10-13**

Jesus touched a leper that no one else would touch and made him clean. **Matthew 8:2-3**

Jesus took a man with dropsy into his hands and healed him. **Luke 14:4**

(This list can be found on our Resource page at wecollide.net/resources)

Jesus Touched a deaf mute, a blind man, an epileptic boy, a woman bent over by a crippling spirit, and a leper no one else would touch, and He healed them all with His hands. These hands that established the heavens and the earth and created you and me, these hands that sculpted the mountains and molded the deserts, the oceans, the rain forests and the glaciers, these hands that made the sparrow and the chameleon, the lily and the rose, the cocoon and the butterfly, these hands that made your hands, these hands that rescued, delivered, and empowered, these hands that hold all power, all truth and all might, they also LOVE. These hands, they entered the place they made. They broke bread and ate with those they created. These hands, they touched the mess no one else would. These hands wanted restoration, sight, and freedom. These hands were willing to bring healing to others at their very own expense. These hands, they were nailed onto a cross, the right stretched out onto a beam and the left. These hands said, and say, over and over again,

I made you. I LOVE YOU. I'LL HOLD YOU, SUSTAIN YOU, WALK ALONGSIDE YOU AND HEAL YOU. WHOEVER STOLE YOUR VALUE, I WILL GIVE IT BACK. I WILL TAKE ALL THE PAIN, SIN, AND WOUNDS, ALL THAT CAUSES ANXIETY, SO THAT YOU WILL ALWAYS KNOW JUST HOW VALUED AND *cared for you are.*

The same hands that made you, save you and promise to keep being all that you need.

Reflect

As you read all that God's hands have done throughout history in Scripture, what stands out to you?

How do you see God's Hand moving around you?

What fascinates you about a God who saw us taking matters into our own hands to relieve our worries so He came and took matters into His own hands?

Go back again to your hand drawing on page 44. Look at the ways you said you try and rescue yourself from worry and fear. In the ways that you have taken matters into your own hands, which can you honestly place in God's? Take time to hand those over by writing them on the Hand below that represents God's.

God's Hand reminds us that He is alive and well. Allow Him to be alive and well in your life!

THE SAME HANDS THAT *made* YOU, *save* YOU AND *promise* TO KEEP BEING ALL THAT YOU NEED.

My husband and I were enjoying a lovely dinner with another couple and over the course of the night my friend, who I mentioned earlier, shared about the difficulty of losing her mom when she was eleven. She remembers her mom going in for surgery. In her kid mind, she thought it meant hope of her mom getting better. Her mom never came out of that surgery. My friend began vulnerably sharing how losing her mom at such a young age affected her.

Just this year she started counseling to process it. She decided she wanted to see her mother's medical records. She accessed the thirty year old documents and almost couldn't believe what she saw. The doctors had written comments about her beautiful mom blessing the hospital staff. She was full of joy AND full of cancer. It had spread all over her body. My friend wasn't told that as a kid. As a kid she was sure that surgery had a shot at saving her mom. But here at 40 she was finding out that her mom knew the surgery had no chance of saving her life and yet she still chose to undergo it in the hopes to extend her life, even if for the shortest of time, to be with her daughter. These medical records told my friend how much her mom was willing to go through: poking, prodding, needles, sickness, going under the knife, all to be with her kid.

The same God who gave my friend this gift to know how valued she is, is the same God who hands over His medical records to all of us so we can see just how valued we are. This God who had healed others chose to relinquish the power He had to save Himself. He chose to be poked, prodded, stripped down, mocked, manhandled, whipped, flogged and pierced, all so that you and I would know what great lengths He would go to for us.
This God says if you've ever wondered how much you are valued, how much you are loved, how much you are cared for, here you go,

LOOK AT THE *cross,* MY MEDICAL RECORD.

Reflect

When you think about my friend hearing how much her mother valued her that she would choose to undergo suffering to be with her daughter just a little longer, what do you think seeing her mother's medical records did for her?

In the same way, what do God's medical records regarding the suffering He chose to undergo do for you? What does the cross tell you about How God feels about you?

Write down the statements you hear God saying to you when you look at His medical records:

I will do anything for you

How can these statements carry you on days when you are worried sick, stressed out and acting out of fear?

Ruminate

Read **Matthew 27:27-50**. As you read this passage, consider your God is doing this so that you know just how much He values you.

Never doubt. Never question. Never second guess. God values you more than He values His own life. When someone wants to steal your value, you fight for it because God already proved it's worth fighting for. To be a woman of faith is not to never make mistakes, or stress out or struggle. To have faith in the midst of worry is to look those things square in the eye and decide to believe, claim, and place all your bets on this one thing:

My God values me.

When some lady at a spa rubs lavender oil on your toes and your mind races about all the ways you might fail, finding God in the midst of worry looks like laying on a massage table and claiming, "**My God values me!**" Reach out to the One bigger than you and call on God to be who God says He is. God reveals who He is in Scripture and you can go looking for Him to be who He promises to be. You can say to your God, "You, God are a God who promises good, redemption, peace, forgiveness, love. You, God have a plan for my life. You are a God who doesn't write stories that end in failure. You actually wrote the very best Story and it ends in victory. (**1 Corinthians 15**) So, God I am counting on You to write a story of victory out of my life, even when I fail."

When your kids are distraught by worry, finding God looks like coming alongside them in their fret and demanding belief out of yourself by claiming what is true, "**My God values me!**" And instead of just preaching all the "right" things they need to do to succeed or make things better, you get down on your knees. Bend over the side of their bed when they lay there stressed out and you go looking for God. It's okay to humble yourself to the place as a parent where you actually admit you have no idea how to make things better and that, actually, all your attempts might not be enough. It's okay to say as a parent to your child, "We need Something bigger than ourselves." Then go looking for God with your kid… "God we come to You for help. We don't know what we are doing or how to make this better. But God we trust that You do. Your ways are higher than our ways. (**Isaiah 55**) Will You guide us? Will You show us what to do? Will You be powerful? We are looking for You. We are Your kids and we need You."

⁵⁵ "WHERE, O DEATH, IS YOUR VICTORY? WHERE, O DEATH, IS YOUR STING?" ⁵⁶ THE STING OF DEATH IS SIN, AND THE POWER OF SIN IS THE LAW. ⁵⁷ BUT THANKS BE TO GOD! HE GIVES US THE VICTORY THROUGH OUR LORD JESUS CHRIST. 1 CORINTHIANS 15:55-57

129

AS THE HEAVENS ARE HIGHER THAN THE *earth*, SO ARE MY WAYS HIGHER THAN YOUR WAYS AND MY THOUGHTS HIGHER THAN YOUR *Thoughts*. ISAIAH 55:9

When you are experiencing a job change and you have no idea what's next and worry already has you convinced that you will soon be homeless, unable to pay your mortgage, working some lame job you're overqualified for, while applying for a thousand jobs and getting none because you were born before 1990… finding God looks like insisting, "**My God values me!**" Then go searching for Him with the same ferocity you've brought to the job market. When you don't know "what's next," go finding God- He knows. You can call upon Him and say… "God, You know all things. You even know what is best for me. God will You show me what is next? Help me not to force, coerce, manufacture or manipulate a direction for my life that isn't Yours. God, You are a come alongside, personal, intervening, alive and well God (**Matthew 1**). You are a God who shows up, runs into and collides with people, collide with me and be my What's Next."

"**My God values me!**" This needs to be your mantra, your pep talk, your heart cry, your insistence. Do not move from it, do not doubt it, do not give any opposing message a half a second chance to breathe. Jesus says when you worry, look at the birds, look at the lilies. The birds and the lilies they remind you that your God values you. This truth is what promises to free you from all that chokes you. God showed you with His life and His death that there is nothing more He values…. than you. Grasp it, own it, claim it and never let it go.

Respond

Take some time today to do just that. Grasp, own, and claim just how much this God values you. Take some time to reflect on God's medical records as seen on the cross and respond to Him as you feel so led.

GRASP HOW MUCH GOD VALUES YOU. OWN IT,

CLAIM IT, AND

Never let it go

Your Story

Kellie

We encourage women to bravely and authentically tell their stories as they really are. We hope this "your story" meets you in yours.

At the age of 28, I gave birth to my first son. I was totally and completely smitten and immediately absorbed in the thrill of having a tiny infant. My pregnancy had been extremely difficult due to a constant migraine headache, nausea and vomiting through the second trimester, and pre-term labor and bed rest in the third. So, waking up every three hours to nurse and jostle my little screamer felt like a cake walk.

When he was about 9 months old, my husband and I packed him up with as much baby paraphernalia as we could carry on a plane and headed to California to visit my sister and her new husband. Although I honestly don't recall much from that trip to California, I'll never forget a conversation I had with my sister that would deeply influence the next 10 years of my life. I was about to begin a painful and worried preoccupation with food and body. My sister had always been thinner than I was. "Stocky" was the term my family used to describe my body-type and although I somehow knew I wasn't the "pretty one" I was resigned to it. We all have our role in our families; hers was to be pretty and mine was to make sure that we held together.

During this visit, my pretty sister was trying to find some of her bigger spare clothes for me to borrow and I was having more than the usual trouble squeezing myself into them. I remember saying in a perky voice, "I know I've got a stomach now, but I've had a baby and I'm okay with it." She sneered and said, "I think you are just making excuses for yourself." I received her statement with such innocent shock. I never saw that coming. As I look back I feel genuine compassion for my vulnerable then-self that travelled back to Washington with a new invisible body wound. Although most girls have been on their first diet by age 11, that wasn't my story. Cheetos were my jam. And jam was my jam. I ate whatever I wanted whenever I wanted it. I didn't know how to calculate a calorie or what one did to burn one. But, the days of worry-free eating and getting dressed in the morning were about to change.

Like so many women before and after me, I fell fast and hard into a daily anxiety over body insecurity and I devoted myself to the task of grasping for the illusory 'good enough' when it came to my appearance. As those initial pounds fell off I was suddenly noticed. People started telling me how good I looked. I think I was terrified of losing the approval I had never known I was missing. With worried vigilance I recommitted to never "make excuses for myself" when back at church after giving birth to my second son a man came up to me and asked, "So…have you lost all the weight yet?"

I think that when Jesus invites us in **Matthew 6** to seek first His kingdom, He is giving the antidote to any variety of worry or anxious distress. Jesus clarifies the nature of our spiritual hunger and offers the path to real nourishment. We are hungry for the kingdom and kingdom-ways. Because of this, we are vulnerable to worry when our focus and priorities are out of alignment with what is actually important. It doesn't matter whether we have become anxious about our size and shape, our bank account, our health, our reputation, or our relationship status, it's the wrong focus. The more energy we pour into our idol of self-interest, the more it fuels the anxious distress. And without a critical realignment of priorities in keeping with His kingdom, our anxious distress then becomes the fuel for our fixation... in a never ending cycle.

On the other hand, serenity is our birthright in Christ.

Align your focus and priorities with His kingdom and what is right under His reign and anxious distress and worry can be replaced with serenity. The audacity of His grace is that when we prioritize loving Him and worshiping Him (**Matthew 22:37**) rather than the idol of our peculiar self-interest, we are given what we really need…and more. Maybe not what we think we need, but certainly the serenity that we need in and out of all circumstances.

Talking with friends, educating yourself, receiving prayer, working with a compassionate therapist, proper nutrition and medication support can be indispensable resources on the road of recovery from worry and anxiety. So is the Holy Spirit. A turning point for me in my worry about what I would eat came when I was reading in the Old Testament how Moses travelled up Mount Sinai after leading the Israelites out of slavery in Egypt. God had just split the Red Sea allowing them to walk through on dry land, He had confused the Egyptian chariots and He had been delivering daily bread out of no-where to feed them! But while Moses was receiving the 10 commandments, the people decide to make a statue of a golden cow to worship. They worship this piece of shiny instead of the living God who had seen their distress while in bondage in Egypt, was compelled by His compassion for them and was providing just what they needed. As I'm reading I'm thinking, "What kind of idiot creates something with their own hands and then worships it?"

In a split second I heard that still small voice inside that said, "You're that kind of idiot."

Oh the bitter-sweet taste of conviction.

In my own self-interest, believing the lie that I would be at peace if I could hang onto being somebody by being a no-body I had become guilty of crafting through diet and exercise an image that I was sacrificing way too much for. I don't think I'm exaggerating when I say that this misalignment of my priorities away from seeking first His kingdom was killing me spiritually, emotionally and relationally.

I have learned and am still learning that seeking His kingdom and righteousness requires constant realignment. This is especially so in the beginning. But it's worth it. As **Psalm 34:8** reminds us, *"Taste and see that the Lord is good; blessed is the one who takes refuge in him."* When we put Jesus back on the throne and seek His kingdom, it becomes the antidote to the worry that wears a thousand different faces.

Written by Kellie Furlan

133

SEEK FIRST

Read

[31] "Therefore do not be anxious, saying, 'What shall we eat?' or 'What shall we drink?' or 'What shall we wear?' [32] For the Gentiles seek after all these things, and your heavenly Father knows that you need them all. [33] But seek first the kingdom of God and his righteousness, and all these things will be added to to you. [34] Therefore do not be anxious about tomorrow, for tomorrow will be anxious for itself. Sufficient for the day is its own trouble." **Matthew 6:31-34 (ESV)**

When we shift our perspective, as Jesus suggests, and look at everything coming from a deep place of knowing our value, we see differently. Worry and fear fade and freedom and hope thrive. When we know we are valued by God, we trust He will come through. When we know we are cared for by God, we bank on God providing all that we need. But it's when we have a deep inner doubt that we are worthy enough of God's care, provision and efforts, that we begin to fret, panic, and stress. As we have seen, Jesus connects value with worry and we ought too, as well.

Jesus wraps up His message on worry with some closing remarks. He basically says, "Don't fret about 'what' will happen or 'what' will not happen. Everyone does that but you, you should be different. You should hang your hat on your heavenly Father who knows what you need."

You know, I think back to a long time ago...to that night, as a 10 year old girl, afraid in my bed about what might happen when a man who had hurt me before broke into our house and I was home alone. I think about that and you know what I needed? I needed my dad. I needed my dad to be there to defend me, to tuck me in, to keep me from my life's circumstances that instilled so much fear in me. But he wasn't. I have spent decades processing the absence, and on occasion presence, of my father. My dad and I have, years later, come to a place of understanding and forgiveness and even friendship. But I often find, that even still, I don't know how to be a daughter to a dad. The idea of trusting a father to know what I need is not instinctual for me. And maybe it's not for you.

Trusting a Father means trusting His character - that He is good, kind, patient, loving. Trusting a Father looks like trusting He's got your back. Trusting a Father requires being sure He will show up on time, pay the bills and keep His word. A trustworthy Father is who He says He is. A trustworthy Father protects. A trustworthy Father shows up. I think it's very easy to miss in this sermon on worry, that Jesus is calling us to recognize that we have a Father who knows what we need.

137

Reflect

Read verses 31 and 32 again. Scripture says you have a heavenly Father who knows what you need. Do you know how to be a daughter to a Dad you can trust? What gets in the way, sometimes, of you being a trusting daughter?

I walked into church one day and my good buddy Ron introduced a new song called "Good Good Father" by Housefires. You should listen to it. It's gorgeous. Ron likes to teach the congregation a song before they sing it. I think this is his way of inviting us all into actually meaning what we sing rather than just going through the church motions like religious robots. So, Ron was doing his thang and started strumming to this song and all of the voices began to chime in around me singing these words…

YOU'RE A GOOD good Father
IT'S WHO YOU ARE
IT'S WHO YOU ARE
IT'S WHO YOU ARE

AND I AM loved by you
IT'S WHO I AM
IT'S WHO I AM
IT'S WHO I AM

YOU ARE PERFECT IN all of your ways
YOU ARE PERFECT IN ALL OF YOUR WAYS
YOU ARE PERFECT IN ALL OF YOUR WAYS
To us

As I put voice to these lyrics, I started weeping. The tears were streaming down my cheeks and I looked like Tammy Faye Baker in the middle of church, but I needed these words. I ate them ravenously, like I was starving. This song identifies our Father and as I sang it, it identified me. "You are a good Father. It's who You are. And I am loved by You. It's who I am." As I wept, I prayed, "Teach me how to be a daughter. Help every cell of my body to believe I am loved by You… That it's who I am. Because it's who You are." And I have prayed that prayer more times than any of you want to know.

Identifying God as a good Father requires identifying yourself as His daughter. Friend, there has been way too much pain and confusion in life and sometimes we lose sense of who we are and Whose we are. You know who you are? You are the daughter of the very best Father. He's got your back. He adores you. You are on His mind and He delights to give you what you need.

Reflect

Go back through and read the lyrics or, preferrably, listen to this song on YouTube (It's called "Good Good Father" by Housefires). What keeps you from believing you have a good Father?

IDENTIFYING GOD AS A *good* FATHER REQUIRES IDENTIFYING YOURSELF AS *His* DAUGHTER.

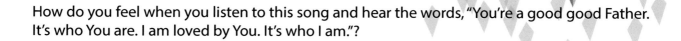

How do you feel when you listen to this song and hear the words, "You're a good good Father. It's who You are. I am loved by You. It's who I am."?

Jesus says our Dad knows what we need. In the table below, spend time writing down what you need and what you want.

Needs	Wants

Now, go back up and circle what your Heavenly Father knows about according to **Matthew 6:32.**

AND MY GOD WILL *meet all your needs* ACCORDING TO THE RICHES OF HIS GLORY IN CHRIST JESUS.

PHILIPPIANS 4:19

Our Father knows what we need and will meet our needs but He also promises to be more than a Dad who works a job to put dinner on the table.

Ruminate

Read the following verses and circle what is most encouraging to you about this Father when it comes to your needs and your wants.

- *May he give you the desire of your heart and make all your plans succeed.* **Psalm 20:4**

- *Take delight in the Lord, and he will give you the desires of your heart.* **Psalm 37:4**

- *You open your hand and satisfy the desires of every living thing.* **Psalm 145:16**

- *And we know that in all things God works for the good of those who love him, who have been called according to his purpose.* **Romans 8:28**

- *If you, then, though you are evil, know how to give good gifts to your children, how much more will your Father in heaven give good gifts to those who ask him!* **Matthew 7:11**

- *He who did not spare his own Son, but gave him up for us all—how will he not also, along with him, graciously give us all things?* **Romans 8:32**

We have a Father who knows what we need and what we want. And we have a Father who knows if we need what we want. Rest in that, my friend.

Fill in the blank to remind yourself of what is true:

We have a Dad who gives us the _____ of our heart.

If earthly parents like to give good gifts to their kids _____ much

_____ will our heavenly Father give us good gifts!

Our Father didn't spare His _____ _____, how

generous is He to shower us with all things!

Jesus says seek first. Here are some words to describe what that word means.

s e e k :

TO *resort* TO

go TO

GO IN *search* OF

look FOR

TO TRY TO *discover*

TO *ask* FOR

request

TO TRY TO *acquire* OR *gain*

aim AT

TO MAKE AN *attempt*

try

"To seek" is the Greek word: **zētéō**; meaning; *to seek after, look for, strive to find.*[25]

When you are stressed out, when you want to bite someone's head off, when you think you can't make it another day, when you are in a spa for your birthday and you are freaking out about everything you need to do, SEEK first.

Not call all your friends and talk trash.
Not go out and beer over it.
Not panic and start a smear campaign.
Not send an email you will regret the next day.
Not uber plan your kid's social life so they have one.
Not Google your hypothetical health scare.
Not frantically prepare for the worst.
Not break up before they dump you.
Not read every piece of propaganda your fear feeds upon.
Not spend hours over analyzing all your next moves.

Seek first God's kingdom.

God's kingdom is the world in which God's ways rule and reign. Seek that kingdom, not this one. This world lies. It covers everything in pleather and fool's gold and calls it pure. This world always tries to get you to be something you're not, making you think it will be then, that you will arrive. And then you get "there" and you still feel empty. This world tells women they are only beautiful if… This world sells you like a product on a shelf. This world sums up a life of success by numbers in a bank account. This world and its power structures set up hierarchies we strive to climb so we can look down upon others to feel good about ourselves. This world has us like hamsters on hamster wheels showing up every day to run hard and fast in the hopes of gaining what we never will. This world glorifies fame and fortune and negates character and integrity. This world exalts greed and mocks humility. This world has us running ragged, worried sick and stressed out because it's trying to rule and reign our lives in a way that can only end in anxiety.

I love how Frederick Buechner describes God's kingdom...

"If we only had eyes to see and ears to hear and wits to understand, we would know that the Kingdom of God in the sense of holiness, goodness, beauty is as close as breathing and is crying out to born both within ourselves and within the world; we would know that the Kingdom of God is what we all of us hunger for above all other things even when we don't know its name or realize that it's what we're starving to death for. The Kingdom of God is where our best dreams come from and our truest prayers. We glimpse it at those moments when we find ourselves being better than we are and wiser than we know. We catch sight of it when at some moment of crisis a strength seems to come to us that is greater than our own strength. The Kingdom of God is where we belong. It is home, and whether we realize it or not, I think we are all of us homesick for it."[26]

25 Zodhiates, Dr. Spiros, editor. *The Complete Word Study Dictionary: New Testament.* reissue ed., AMG Publishers, 1992.
26 Buechner, Frederick. *Secrets in the Dark: A Life in Sermons.* Reprint ed., Harper Collins, 2009.

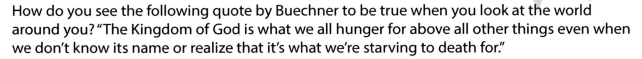

Reflect

How do you see the following quote by Buechner to be true when you look at the world around you? "The Kingdom of God is what we all hunger for above all other things even when we don't know its name or realize that it's what we're starving to death for."

I love how Buechner says, "The Kingdom of God is where we belong." Where have you been trying to belong?

Do you fit where you have been trying to belong?

How has the world been lying to you about who and what reigns and rules because it has been promising to bring you the peace your worry longs for?

Jesus says, "Seek first God's kingdom." How can you attempt first in your worry and fear to belong to God's kingdom?

Jesus is inviting us to look for God's kingdom which looks different than this worldly one. This worldly one has our worry convinced that it's who has all the rule and reign. Jesus is calling us to seek something More, something Bigger, something Better, something Now and something Coming when we are worried and anxious. He is calling His followers to trust that God is real and God's kingdom reigns no matter what your circumstances tell you! Jesus is asking us to be women, who in Chapter 7, wait for the end of the story and how it plays out. With Jesus things don't compute like we think they will. One and one don't make two. A loss is often a win. And a win in this worldly kingdom can be a loss in God's. Death looks like death to us, but to Jesus it looks like resurrection. In Jesus' kingdom things aren't always what they seem. The world's ways are not God's ways. So hold on because though your circumstances find you expecting the worst, God seems to say, "Expect the Unexpected, I'm coming. Look for Me. "

Seek.

Reflect

How does your worry convince you that the world and its ways reign over God and His ways?

DEATH LOOKS LIKE DEATH TO US, BUT TO JESUS IT LOOKS LIKE

resurrection.

How do you find yourself in what might actually be Chapter 7 of your life, not trusting God for the whole story?

How are you comforted right now in a God whose reign and rule can take a loss and make it the ultimate victory? And in the same way, how are you comforted that what looks like a win in the world might be a loss in God's kingdom?

Before all the other things we tend to do when we worry, before taking matters into our own hands, Jesus says "seek."

Acts 17:24-28 says, *24"The God who made the world and everything in it is the Lord of heaven and earth and does not live in temples built by human hands.25 And he is not served by human hands, as if he needed anything. Rather, he himself gives everyone life and breath and everything else.26 From one man he made all the nations, that they should inhabit the whole earth; and he marked out their appointed times in history and the boundaries of their lands. 27 God did this so that they would seek him and perhaps reach out for him and find him, though he is not far from any one of us. 28 'For in him we live and move and have our being.' As some of your own poets have said, 'We are his offspring."*

WE WERE *made* TO *seek.*

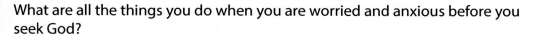
Reflect

What are all the things you do when you are worried and anxious before you seek God?

Why do you think seeking isn't always first on your list of responses?

What do you find fascinating about the idea that you are in this very place at this very time, made to seek God?

What does **Acts 17:27** say will happen when you seek God?

Scripture connects the very reason for us being here at this time and this place is to seek, reach out and find our heavenly Father who made us in the first place. Seeking God in the midst of worry looks like saying, "You first," to a God who already said that to us with His life. God's hand is already outstretched toward us, wanting to provide, intervene, guide, comfort, heal and rescue. God's hand reaches out to you and has already said, "You first." It seems like He hopes we will do the same, reaching out our hand, looking to grasp His, saying "You first, before all other things.'"

Our most beautiful response to our heavenly Father is to stretch out our hands in His direction and receive His love and care. The same God who shaped you with His hands, sculpted you in your mother's womb, architecturally designed your destiny, penned your chapters - that same God opens His hand and waits for you to reach out your hand and grab His.

HE DOES, *after all,* *know* WHAT YOU *need.*

Respond

Let's end this experience by opening our hands, palms up. Pray along with me…

Lord Jesus, thank You for colliding with me, as worried and stressed as I can be. Thank You for coming into my mess and my pain and bringing about more healing and freedom in my life. I hand You all the ways I have taken matters into my own hands and I now lean into You to be my Rescuer, my Sustainer, my Provider and my perfect Father. Help me to be Your daughter, trusting You each and every day. When worry and fear try to overcome, be victorious. I will look at the birds and the lilies to be reminded of just how much You value and care for me. I desire to seek You first before all other things. Thank you for being a God who pursues me and with Your life, puts me first.

Amen

"THEREFORE DO NOT BE *anxious* ABOUT *tomorrow*,
FOR *tomorrow* WILL BE *anxious* FOR ITSELF.
SUFFICIENT FOR THE *day* IS ITS OWN TROUBLE."

MATTHEW 6:34 ESV

What an accomplishment! You did it! You walked through an arduous, soul working process of seeking the Lord to meet you in your worry and your anxiety! We want to bless you. Our designer and resident artist, Lindsey, who so beautifully crafted this study has designed an art print just for you. Email us at info@wecollide.net and send us a shout-out letting us know that you finished this study! In return we will send you updates on Collide and future bible studies, and we'll email you a free downloadable art print that will remind you of the work God did in you through this experience! Hope to hear from you soon!

LEADER
GUIDE

Friends!

I cannot express how much I think leading a group of women centering around a passage of Scripture where Jesus collides, will change lives! Your sacrifice, investment, service and care of these women has the capacity to change their family lives, their friendships, their stress and anxiety, their dreams and their sense of purpose! We cannot wait to hear the ways Jesus collides with you and your gathering of women as you walk them through this study! We have put together a 90-minute experience you can walk women through each time you meet together, covering each part of the study. Please be prayerful, give yourself grace and feel free to cut, edit or add to the experience as you feel so led! If you hate a question we suggest, skip it. If you think of some fun engaging activity that will add to your group's experience, do it! We trust that God is leading you and we merely give you this leader's guide as a tool to use as you see best. May God collide with you as you invite others to collide with Him!

Section 1

THE ANXIETY EPIDEMIC

Supplies needed:
Bible Study and Bible
Whiteboard or large
Piece of paper
Markers

LEADER (15 minutes)

Welcome!

Invite each woman to introduce herself by answering the following 3 questions:

- *What is your name?*
- *Why are you excited to be here?*
- *What is the silliest way you have seen someone comfort themselves when stressed? (perhaps in real life, or in a movie or tv series)*

GROUP (15 minutes)

Read Matthew 6:19-34

Reflect

- *What are some of the things from this passage of scripture that immediately jump out at you?*
- *How do you resonate with Willow's spa experience?*
- *Call out some of the ways from p. 13 that worry presents itself in your life.*

PARTNER (5 minutes)

Reflect

- Split into groups of 2 or 3 and discuss the first reflection question on p. 14.

GROUP (20 minutes)

Ruminate

- Ask several women to take turns reading aloud the statistics on p. 15.

Reflect

- *Which of these statistics do you relate to most?*
- Discuss answers to the first two reflection questions on p. 16.
- **Activity** – Use a whiteboard or large piece of paper and invite women to come up and write other statements we are often told when we exhibit anxious or stressful feelings. (For example: You must be about to start your period.) Then, as a group come up with one helpful statement to replace each harmful one. Cross out the harmful statement and write the helpful statement instead.

PARTNER (10 minutes)

Reflect

- Split into groups of 2 or 3. Read the bold parts of the bulleted statements on p. 17 and discuss how you find yourself trying to relieve your own stress and worry. (p.18)

GROUP (15 minutes)

Reflect

- Spend time discussing the Brain Dump exercise on pp. 19-20. Choose some of the questions on p. 21 to help guide your discussion.

LEADER (10 minutes)

Respond

- *Jesus meets us where we are at. Where are you currently at with stress and anxiety? Where do you want to be?*
- Pray aloud for the group, the prayer on p. 23 substituting the word "our" for the word "my".

Section 2

YOU SHOULD BE AFRAID

Supplies needed:
Bible Study and Bible
Whiteboard or large piece of paper
Markers
Phone or computer to play a song

LEADER (10 minutes)

Welcome!

- *Last week we discussed some of the ways we attempt to alleviate our worry and anxiety. How did you catch yourself doing that this week?*

PARTNER (10 minutes)

Reflect

- Split into groups of 2 or 3 and discuss the relationship between worry and fear in your life. (pp. 29-30)

GROUP (25 minutes)

Reflect

- Invite women to share some of their examples of a time fear wrote a hypothetical story in their heads? (p.30)

Read Matthew 6:19-34
Reflect

- *Does anything new jump out at you in this passage in light of what we have already begun discussing?*

Ruminate

- Have several women read aloud the passages on p. 31.
- *When doing the study this week, why did you circle the passages you did and how are you allowing those verses to encourage you?*

PARTNER (10 minutes)

Reflect

- Split into groups of 2 or 3 and share your stories and the 5 different scenarios you came up with?
- Discuss the dangers of letting fear dominate our thinking. (p. 34)

GROUP (10 minutes)

Reflect

- *On p. 35, we see that Jesus is in the business of freeing people. When you read that page this week, whose fear did you most resonate with? The man waiting by the waters to be healed, Martha, the adulteress?*
- *And what is it you see Jesus doing over and over again for people in their fear that brings comfort to you in yours?*
- *Have you had a moment this week where a big or small fear began to creep in and you experienced Jesus' comfort and presence in that fear?*

INDIVIDUAL (5 minutes)

Reflect

- *Spend some time quietly going back over your answers to the questions on pp. 33-34. After looking at the 5 new stories you were able to tell yourself, go back to the question at the bottom of p. 33. Circle only the parts of the story you are telling yourself that you are certain are true.*

GROUP (10 minutes)

Ruminate

- Have several women take turns reading aloud the verses on p. 36, pausing after each one to complete the activity below.
- **Activity** – Use a whiteboard or large piece of paper to list the actions collectively that each woman came up with individually that we can take to walk toward freedom and away from fear.

LEADER (10 minutes)

Respond

- Ask if anyone will bravely share the hymn they wrote.
- Invite women into quiet personal contemplation and prayer as you play the song "His Eye Is on The Sparrow". (Can be found on iTunes or YouTube.)

Section 3
TAKING MATTERS INTO YOUR OWN HANDS

Supplies needed:
Bible Study and Bible
Piece of stationary or blank paper for each woman
Envelopes

LEADER (10 minutes)
Welcome!

- *What are some ways you have noticed other people letting fear creep into their lives?* (remind women to keep confidential matters confidential)
- *What are some ways you noticed fear creeping into your life this week?*

PARTNER (10 minutes)
Reflect

- Split into groups of 2 or 3 and share your hand drawings with each other. (p. 44)
- Discuss the ways you take matters into your own hands.

GROUP (25 minutes)
Reflect

- Discuss the ways our attempts to make everything better create more things to worry about. (p. 45)
- *Why do you think we continue taking matters into our own hands if we know it creates more stress and anxiety?*

Ruminate

- Have several women look up and read aloud the verses on p. 46 and discuss what God has or will rescue His people from.
- *What circumstances in your life prompted you to circle the verses you did?*

PARTNER (15 minutes)

Reflect

- Break into groups of 2 or 3, discuss ways you relate to the story of the "party planner." (pp. 47-49)
- *How do you see her adding to her own anxiety?*
- *What do you want to say to her?*
- *If someone were to make that same statement to you, how would it impact you upon hearing it?*

INDIVIDUAL (15 minutes)

Reflect

- *Spend some time contemplating your answers to the last half of questions on p. 49.*
- **Activity** – Give each woman a piece of stationary or a blank piece of paper. Invite them to write a letter to themselves to bring about encouragement, hope and faith in their deepest desires, greatest anxieties and biggest fears. (Have them put the letters in a self-addressed envelope, collect them and mail them at a later date.)

LEADER (15 minutes)

Respond

- Ask women to share the following:
  - *What do you feel you need rescue from?*
  - *How are you trying to rescue yourself?*
- Lead the group in prayer for these specific things.

Section 4

WHAT DO YOU TREASURE?

Supplies needed:
Bible Study and Bible
Paper or journal for each woman

LEADER (10 minutes)

Welcome!

- *Were there any moments throughout the week where you noticed you were taking matters into your own hands?*

GROUP (10 minutes)

Read Matthew 6:19-24

Reflect

- *Willow gives a warning that this part of Jesus' message might be hard to hear. Why do you think Jesus would begin His sermon on worry by tackling the issue of what we treasure?*

INDIVIDUAL (10 minutes)

Reflect

- Walk the women through the following:
    - (3 minutes) *Take a look at your wishlist on p. 57. In the margin, write what you are hoping those things will add to your life.*
    - (3 minutes) *Now look at the list you wrote on p. 58 of imperishable treasures. In the margin, write what they add to your life.*
    - (4 minutes) *Take time to journal what you notice as you look at your wishlist and your imperishable list.*

GROUP (15 minutes)

Reflect

- Invite women to share what they discovered during their self-reflection time.
- Discuss the reasons women believe we continue to store up treasures that are perishable. (p. 58)
- Read aloud the paragraph at the bottom of p. 58.
- Discuss the question on p. 59.

PARTNER (10 minutes)

Reflect

- In groups of 2 or 3, discuss the questions about generosity on p. 60 and if any of your answers surprised you.

GROUP (15 minutes)

Ruminate

- Read aloud the definitions of what the word money means in this passage of scripture.
- *How do you see us, as people, serving "mammon"?*

PARTNER (10 minutes)

Reflect

- In groups of 2 or 3, discuss the first two questions on p. 62.

LEADER (10 minutes)

Respond

- **Activity** - *Stay in your groups of 2 or 3, and first spend time individually writing to God in prayer, expressing the things you hope to treasure. Then share with your partner(s) what those hopes are and pray for one another.*

Section 5
LOOK AT THE BIRDS

Supplies needed:
Bible Study and Bible
Whiteboard or large piece of paper
Black marker
Red marker

LEADER (10 minutes)
Welcome!

- *This past week, how did you see people tempted to trust their treasures over God?*
- *Were there any times throughout the week where you made a conscious decision to choose God over something else you treasure?*

GROUP (15 minutes)
Read Matthew 6:25-27
Reflect

- **Activity** – Use a whiteboard or large piece of paper. Invite women to come up and write in black marker what they hear when someone says to them, "Do not worry." Encourage women to come up with other examples beyond what we've given on p. 67. (Leave space beneath each statement and leave this up, we'll come back to it later.)
- *How does it make you feel when you hear these statements?*

PARTNER (10 minutes)
Reflect

- In groups of 2 or 3, read p. 68.
- *What do you think is the difference between "prudent" worry and worry that "takes all the joy out of life"?*
- *Barclay suggests that "not worrying ought to come with 'prudence and serenity.'" The definition of the word prudence is: the quality of being prudent; cautiousness. The definition of the word serenity is: the state of being calm, peaceful, and untroubled. How can we carry ourselves with caution and peace?*

GROUP (15 minutes)
Ruminate

- Read aloud Psalm 104:10-23, 27-28 (p. 71).

GROUP (cont'd)

Reflect

- *Read verse 28 again. What happens when God "opens" His hand? (p.71)*
- *How have you seen God's Hand open up and satisfy you with good things, personally?*
- Discuss the two questions on p. 72.

INDIVIDUAL (5 minutes)

Reflect

- *Spend time looking at the list you wrote on p. 73 of the things you are worried God won't sustain. In the margin, write the reasons you think He can't or won't sustain those things.*

GROUP (25 minutes)

Reflect

- *Why do you think we struggle to believe God won't sustain the things we are worried about?*
- Invite women to call out some of the truths they wrote over their hand drawing on p. 44.
- Discuss the questions on p. 74.
- *Can you share an example of a time you encouraged a friend that God would sustain them, yet later, found yourself in a similar situation and had a difficult time believing that for yourself?*

Ruminate

- Ask several women to read aloud the verses on p. 75.
- **Activity** - Go back to the whiteboard or large sheet of paper. In the space you left beneath each one, write a response that trusts that God can and will sustain what it is you worry about. An example would be:
  Get over it.
- Have women cross that out and underneath it write:
  God's got you.
- Invite women to to practice the spiritual art of replacing lame answers and broken lies with truths that bring life and hope.

LEADER (10 minutes)

Respond

- Invite women to share their experiences with the "homework assignment" on p. 77.
- Encourage women to pray out loud, thanking God for how He has sustained them personally and ask Him to sustain what they worry about.

Section 6
LOOK AT THE LILIES

Supplies needed:
Bible Study and Bible
Ten small pieces of colored paper for each woman

LEADER (10 minutes)

Welcome!

- *Last week we talked about how God sustains us. What were some things you noticed this week which further showed you God's sustenance?*

GROUP (20 minutes)

Read Matthew 6:26-31
Reflect

- *How does Jesus compare you to to the lilies?*
- Discuss all the questions on p. 84.

PARTNER (10 minutes)

Reflect

- In groups of 2 or 3, read p. 85 and discuss the impact Jesus' preaching about the lilies would have had on the women of this culture.

GROUP (10 minutes)

Reflect

- *What strikes you about the connection Jesus makes here between worry and value?* (p. 86)

PARTNER (10 minutes)

Reflect

- Spend time sharing with your partner(s) about your 3 biggest worries and how you see yourself questioning your value with those worries. (p. 87)

INDIVIDUAL (10 minutes)

- **Activity** - Give each woman ten small pieces of colored paper and have them write statements of God's value for them. An example would be: "God made me" or "God knows the number of hairs on my head." Spread the papers out on the floor and invite every woman to soak them up.

GROUP (10 minutes)

Reflect

- *What strikes you about what you wrote versus what other women wrote?*
- *Can you own and receive these statements to be true for yourself? Why or why not?*
- *Why do you think you doubt God's value of you?*

LEADER (10 minutes)

Respond

- *The connection Jesus is drawing between worry and value seems so important, so let's take time to pray that we fully grasp it. Take this time to pray for one another other to truly grasp just how much God values us.*
- Give women a warning that Section 7 has a lot to process and it may require a little more time.

Section 7
STOLEN VALUE

Supplies needed:
Bible Study and Bible
Whiteboard or large piece of paper (with the table below)
Marker

LEADER (10 minutes)

Welcome!

- *Last week we began to scratch the surface regarding the connection between worry and value. How did that concept change your perspective this week?*
- *Did any of the statements on the papers from last week that you all wrote come back to bless you?*

GROUP (70 minutes)

Read Matthew 6:19-34

Reflect

- *How does it strike you that our sense of value is perhaps connected to a lot of worry's root and worry's cure?*
- *Which of the 6 ways that our value can get stolen did you most resonate with?*
- Invite women to locate a moment in their lives where their sense of value was stolen. Take time to allow each woman who would like to share a story of when their value was taken from them. As they share, have courage to invite the group to speak truths over each woman individually after she shares. Then pray for her.
- *What do you love about Jesus that He would collide with someone who lost their value and give it back?*

GROUP (cont'd)

Ruminate

- *When you read the passages on p. 105 which story gives you the most hope that God can replace your stolen sense of value?*

Reflect

- Read the bottom paragraph on p 106.
- **Activity** - Invite the women to consider what it is that has stolen their sense of value and what it is they need to begin to believe about God. Then invite them to write their answers on a large piece of paper that has a line through the middle from top to bottom.

Example:

I struggle to believe:	God is:
I struggle to believe God will protect me.	God is my protector.
I struggle to forgive myself	God forgives.

LEADER (10 minutes)

Respond

- Close by ending in prayer, praying that the women will begin to believe more in the statements on the right side of the table than the left side.

Section 8
BACKWARD TO GO FORWARD

Supplies needed:
Bible Study and Bible

LEADER (10 minutes)
Welcome!

- Invite every woman to go around the circle and identify which of the things on p. 114 they find themselves doing when they face hardship. For example: "I pretend they aren't happening." Or "I stay busy so I don't have to face reality."
- Invite them to share why they think they respond to hard things in life this way.

GROUP (45 minutes)
Read Matthew 6:19-34
Reflect

- *What do you think about the idea that you often have to go backward to go forward?*
- Discuss the three questions on p. 115 about sweeping things under the rug.

Ruminate

- Read each verse on pp. 115-116. *What does scripture say will happen with all things that are covered up or hidden?*

GROUP (cont'd)

Reflect

- Read the final paragraph on p. 117 and then discuss the questions on p.118.
- *Do you invite God into…*
    - *your past but not your present?*
    - *your present but not your past?*
    - *only your future?*
- *How hard is it for you to invite God into your mess? Why do you think that is?*
- *When you think about what you know about Jesus, whose mess did He enter into and what did He do when He did?*
- *How does reminding yourself that Jesus entered mess encourage you, that God might enter yours?*

PARTNER (25 minutes)

Reflect

- In groups of 2 or 3, have women share with each other a memory of when their value was taken from them. Have them share what they think they lost and what they needed at the time. Invite them to pray that the Lord restores everything that has been taken.

LEADER (10 minutes)

Respond

- Invite the women to close by holding their hands out, palms facing up and read over them **Deuteronomy 30:3** from The Message: *"God, your God, will restore everything you lost. He'll have compassion on you; He'll come back and pick up the pieces from all the places where you were scattered."*

*Please be sensitive to the painful and deep emotions this section might stir up and adjust your time accordingly. Counseling may be the next step some of these women need. Please refer to p.120 for some great tips about seeking a counselor.

Section 9
GOD TAKES MATTERS INTO
HIS OWN HANDS

Supplies needed:
Bible Study and Bible
Whiteboard or large piece of paper
Marker

LEADER (10 minutes)

Welcome!

- *What did you do with your hands this week?*
- *What do you find interesting about what God has pulled off with His hands?*

GROUP (25 minutes)

Read Matthew 6:19-34
Ruminate

- *Which of the statements on pp. 122-123 encouraged you most this week?*

Reflect

- *What fascinates you about a God who saw us taking matters in your own hands to relive our worries so He came and took matters into His own Hands?*

PARTNER (10 minutes)

Reflect

- In groups of 2 or 3, share what it brought up in you to complete the exercise on p. 125?

GROUP (25 minutes)

Reflect

- Invite women to share what stood out to them about what their partner shared regarding the exercise's impact on them.
- *After reading the story on p. 126 how do you think this woman would have felt upon seeing her mother's medical records?*
- Read Matthew 27:27-50 together.
- *When you think of Jesus' hands being nailed to the cross and you look upon God's "medical records" and what He would do for you, what message do you hear?*
- (**Activity** - write these up on the whiteboard/paper.)
  How can these messages carry each of us through our worry and anxiety?

PARTNER (10 minutes)

Reflect

- *Revisit the "everyday" circumstances on pp. 129-130 where our value can easily be questioned and share with each other an everyday circumstance you have had recently where you began questioning your value. After you share the circumstance, allow your partner to invite you into one or two ways you can combat questioning your value.*
  - For example: your partner might share about her mother-in-law who makes passive aggressive comments regarding her cooking. And you can give her 1-2 helpful ways to remember her God values her in moments like those. Perhaps she could:
    1. Pray and ask God to encourage her in her efforts to serve her in laws.
    2. Remind herself that her value rests outside of any man or woman's opinion of her.

LEADER (10 minutes)

Respond

- Invite women to pray, thanking God for how much He values them as they grasp, own and claim it to be true.

*Leader Note - One of Collide's core values is pushing towards growth and next steps to go further on one's own journey with God. To that end, we always want to make sure we end each of our Bible study groups by presenting women with opportunities to take a "next step." At the end of the next lesson, we will be giving you some of the opportunities available through Collide for women to continue colliding with Jesus. We'd love for you to be thinking about the opportunities available in your area so you can offer some local options as well.

Section 10
SEEK FIRST

Supplies needed:
Bible Study and Bible

LEADER (10 minutes)

Welcome!

- *Do you have a funny story you want to share about a time where you were so focused on one thing that you missed what was happening around you?*
- *When is a time that you can now look back upon and recognize that all you needed was a shift in perspective to get out of a "funk,", bad mood or negative mindset?*
- *What did you do to shift your perspective?*

GROUP (60 minutes)

Read Matthew 6:31-34

Reflect

- *Identifying God as a good Father requires identifying yourself as His daughter. What is hard for you about identifying as God's daughter? What do you love about that identity?*
- *Was there a portion of the lyrics of "Good Good Father" that you want to hold on to?*
- *How did the difference between your needs and wants list strike you?*
- *The list on p. 143 gives some examples of the things we often do rather than seek God when we are stressed and anxious, go back and circle which you resonate with and share with the group.*

GROUP (cont'd)

Ruminate

- *Which of these verses in the ruminate section on p. 141 do you feel you need to hold onto for a specific circumstance in your life right now, and why?*
- *Frederick Buechner says, "...the kingdom of God is what we all of us hunger for above all other things even when we don't know its name or realize it's what we are starving to death for." If God is what we are all starving for, why do you think we often seek everything but Him in moments and seasons of our lives?*
- *What do you think would cause you to seek first instead of second?*

Reflect

- Discuss the last 2 questions on p. 144.
- Read aloud the paragraph on p.145.
- Discuss the questions on p.146.
- *What does Acts 17:27 say will happen when you seek God?*
- *Describe a time when you have experienced being worried and yet you chose to seek God and in that, you found Him?*

LEADER (20 minutes)

Respond

- Invite women to express where they were when they began this study, where they are now, and how they have collided with Jesus and experienced finding Him through this group experience?
- Pray over each woman a blessing to end your time together.
- Please encourage the women to continue colliding with Jesus by letting them know about some local "next step" options as well as these opportunities through Collide:
  - Subscribe to the We Collide Podcast (This can be found at wecollide.net or any major podcasting forum).
  - Choose another Collide Bible study to go through or host your own Bible study group.
  - Spend some time on the Collide blog where you will find engaging content written by everyday women.

come

collide.

with us

we have more ways you can collide

with Jesus at wecollide.net

or find us on

Acknowledgements

This project was a collective work of some amazing women getting together and trusting God could use the sum of what we have to do something big. I am so very grateful for these women who poured out their energy, leaned into their giftings, gave of their time, and made great sacrifices to craft this project and get it into the hands of those we believe it will impact. God calls His people the Body, and as I like to say, God gave Collide one hot body! These beautiful women are the hands and feet, the heart and mind, the lungs and mouthpiece being used to bless the world around them and for that, I am truly grateful. There is nothing greater than together handing God what we have and seeing what He can do!

Willow

Willow Weston, Author *Willow's life is full of crazy, unexpected, broken and beautiful moments that have given way to incredible healing both in her own life and now others. Willow is a sassy, fun, word nerd. She is a spelling bee winner and an eternal 7th grader and is totally fine with it. Willow collided with Jesus and He radically changed her life and now lives to tell everyone else about Him. Willow lives in Bellingham, Washington with her husband of twenty years and her two amazing kiddos. She speaks about God's love at camps, retreats, churches, and other gatherings, in addition to her work as Founder and Director of Collide.*

Michelle Holladay, Content Contributor *Michelle believes passionately in God's word and loves helping others discover how relevant the Bible is to our everyday lives. Her ideal day would be spent on a warm beach with a good book. One day, she blinked and her two children were grown, but being a mom will always be her favorite job, one she has happily shared with her husband of over 25 years. We are so grateful for Michelle's love of God's word that guided her to help shape, research and edit the writing and content portion of this study.*

Lindsey Kiniry, Graphic Designer *Lindsey is a rodeo wrangler, a taxi driver, a chaos manager, and a really terrible chef all rolled into one most days. Though she might seem like the life of the party, this secretly shy gal loves to connect with people one-on-one in a quiet space. Lindsey has a husband, 3 kids, 2 cats, a dog and 8 chickens. Her most favorite moments are in creating something and handing Jesus the paint brush. And boy are we glad that Lindsey does because God continues to use her gifts and did so to create the art in this study that so beautifully draws us into Him.*

Anna Kuttel, Project Manager *Anna seeks to be authentic by entering into others' joy, hurt, and mess. Anna's background is composed of such seemingly paradoxical passions and experiences as anthropology and interior design, real estate and nonprofit, all of which have shaped her into a continually learning-and-growing wife, a mom of two strong and joyful young boys, and a Collide staff extraordinaire. We are ever thankful to Anna for the way she thinks, organizes, administrates and keeps us all in line- this project needed her gifts to make dreams become reality!*

Made in the USA
Monee, IL
20 September 2020